Emily™
the Strange

by Cosmic Debris

CHRONICLE BOOKS
SAN FRANCISCO

Illustrated by Buzz Parker, Brian Brooks, and Rob Reger
www.emilystrange.com

Library of Congress Cataloging-in-Publication Data available.

ISBN 0-8118-3147-7
Printed in Singapore

Distributed in Canada by Raincoast Books
9050 Shaughnessy Street
Vancouver, British Columbia V6P 6E5

10 9 8 7 6 5 4 3 2

Chronicle Books LLC
85 Second Street
San Francisco, California 94105
www.chroniclebooks.com

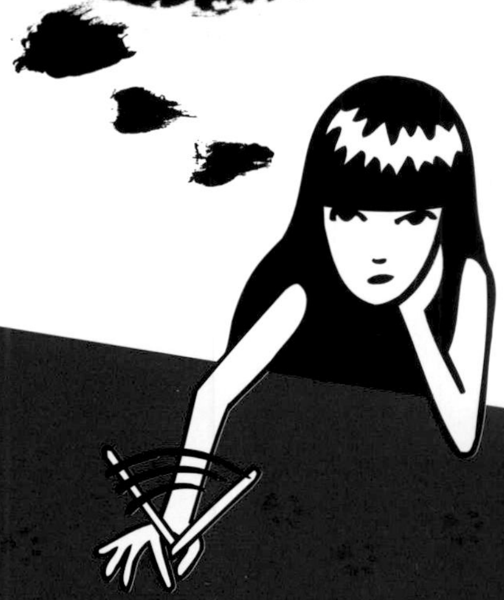

for

HUMES

the "Human Cat"

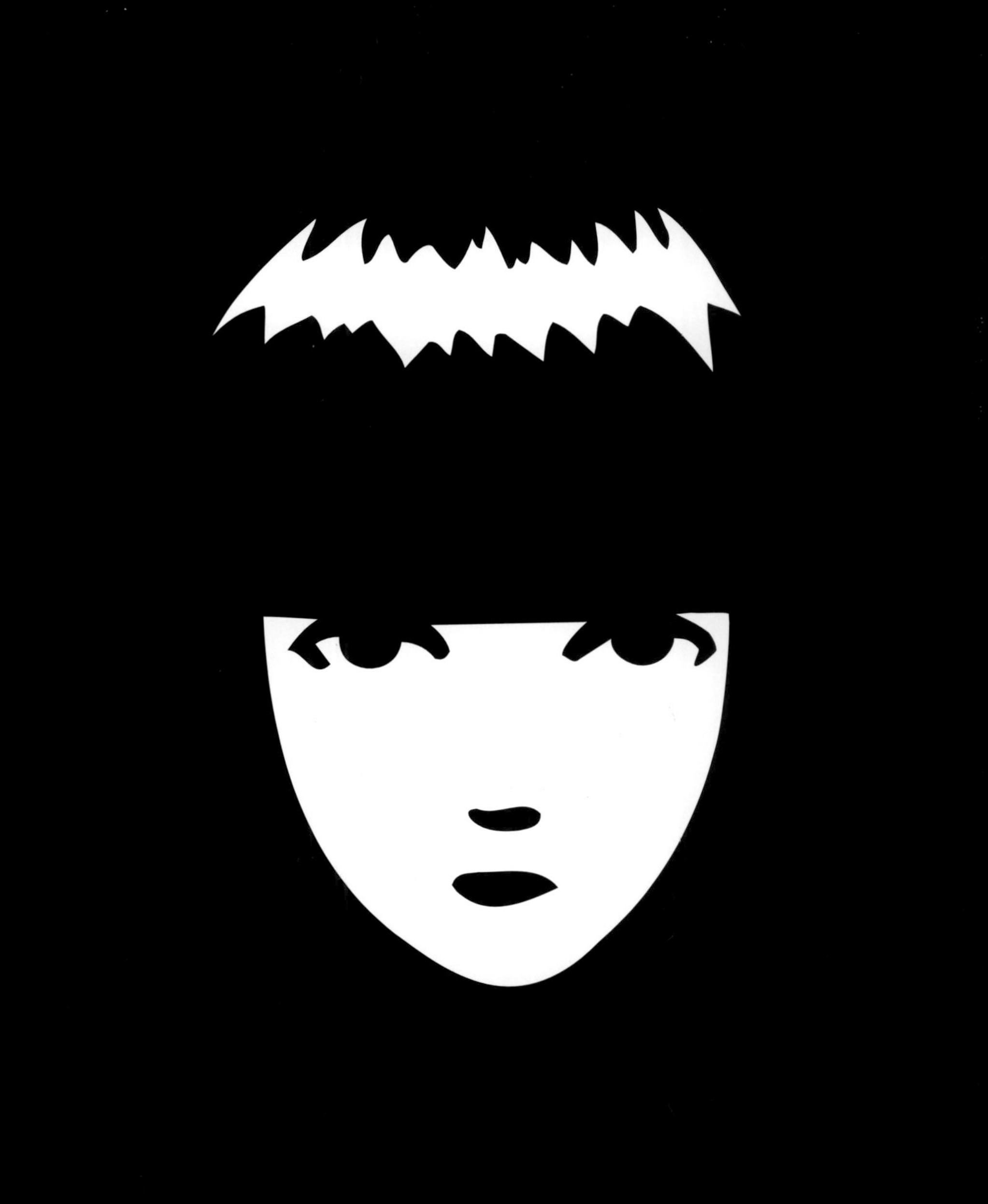

Emily doesn't search to belong...

...she searches to be lost.

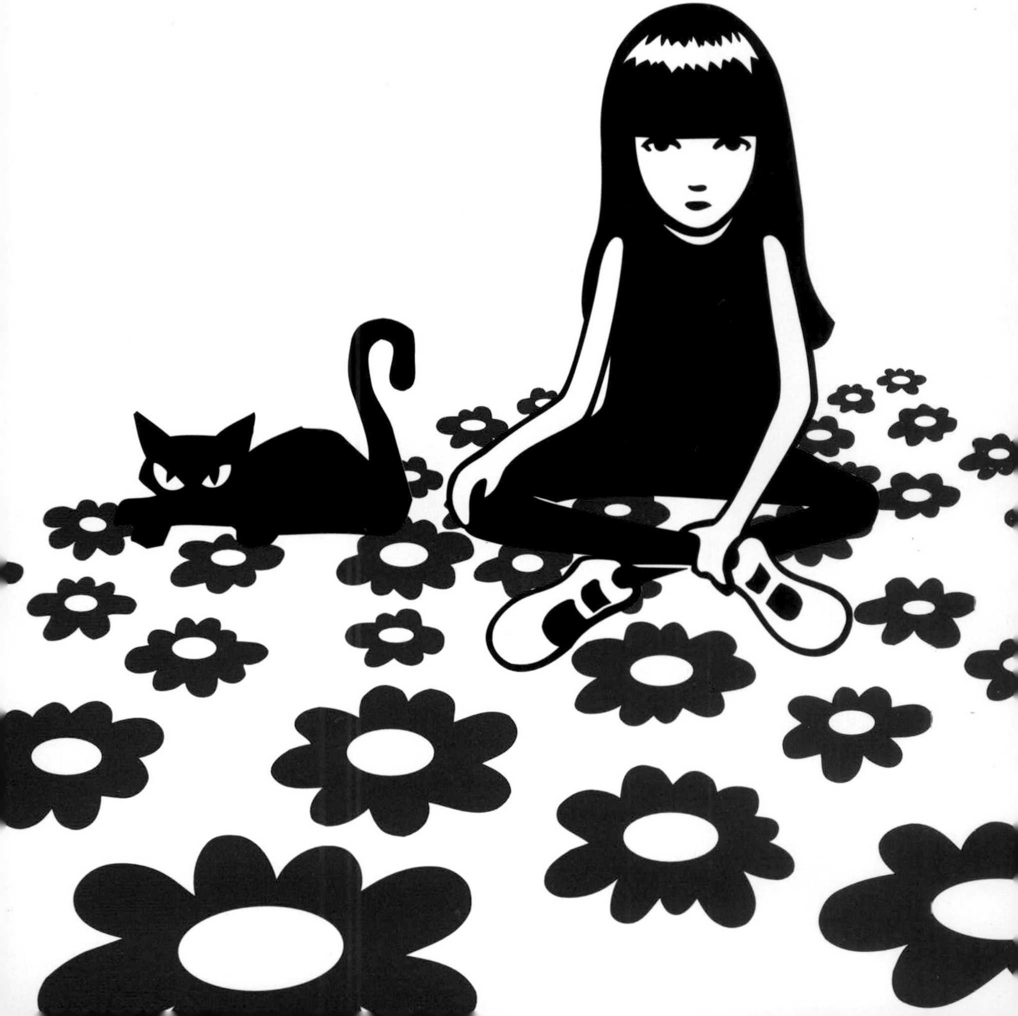

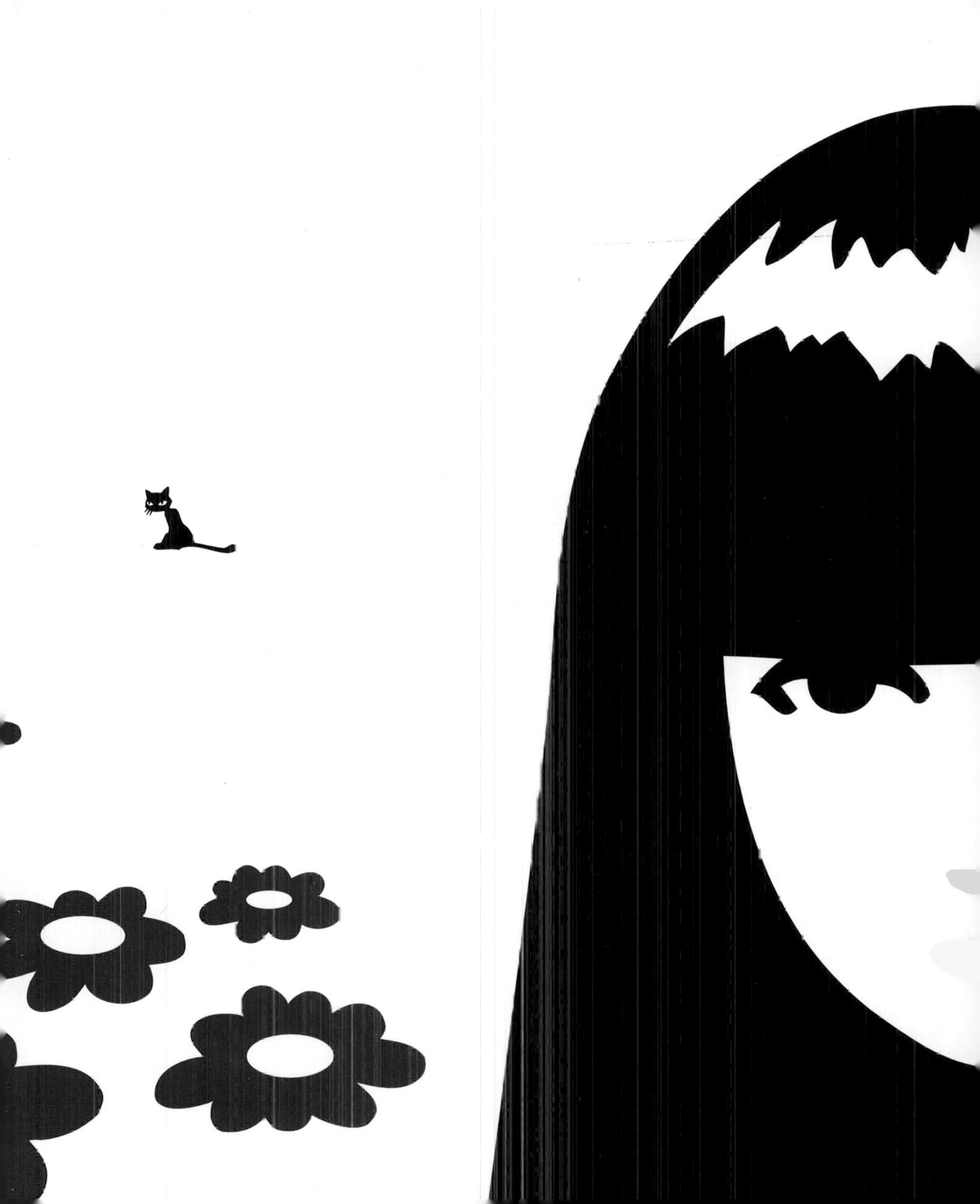

Get lost.

Emily isn't lazy...

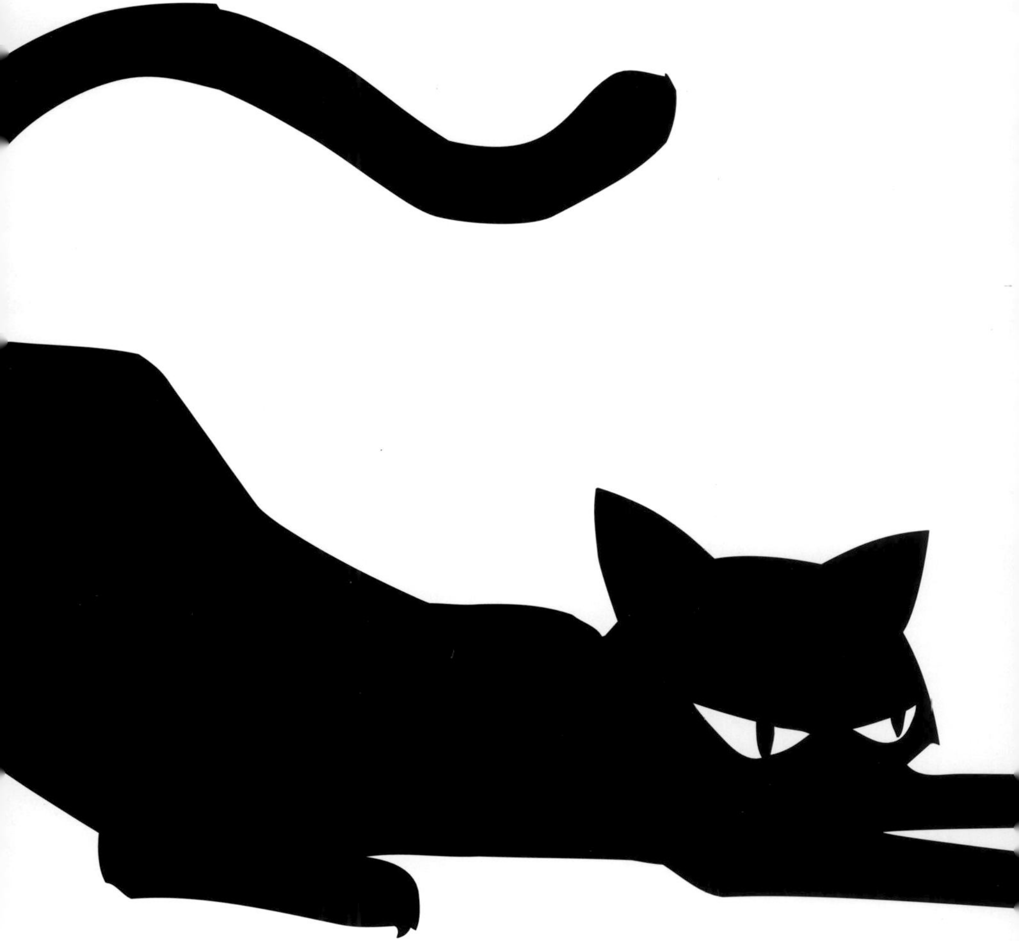

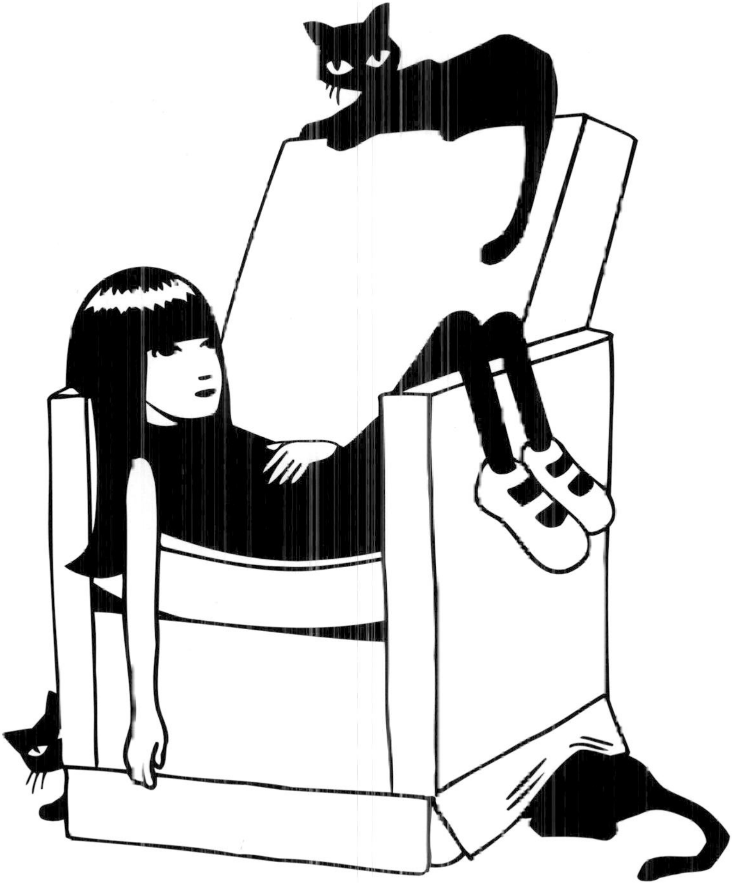

...she's just happy doing nothing.

Emily believes...

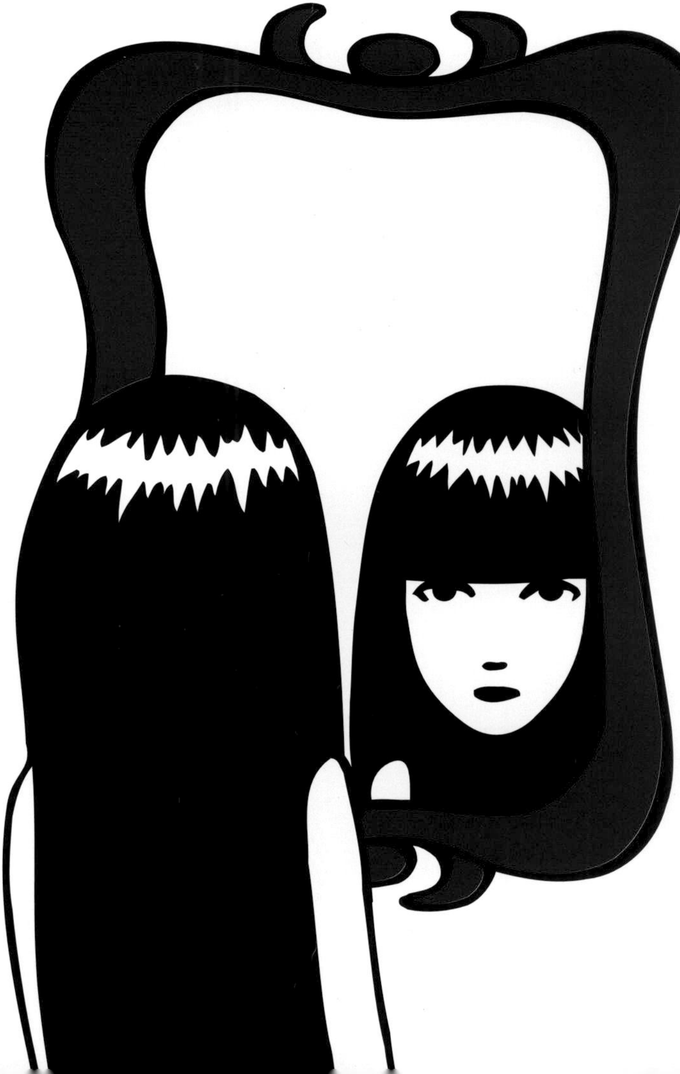

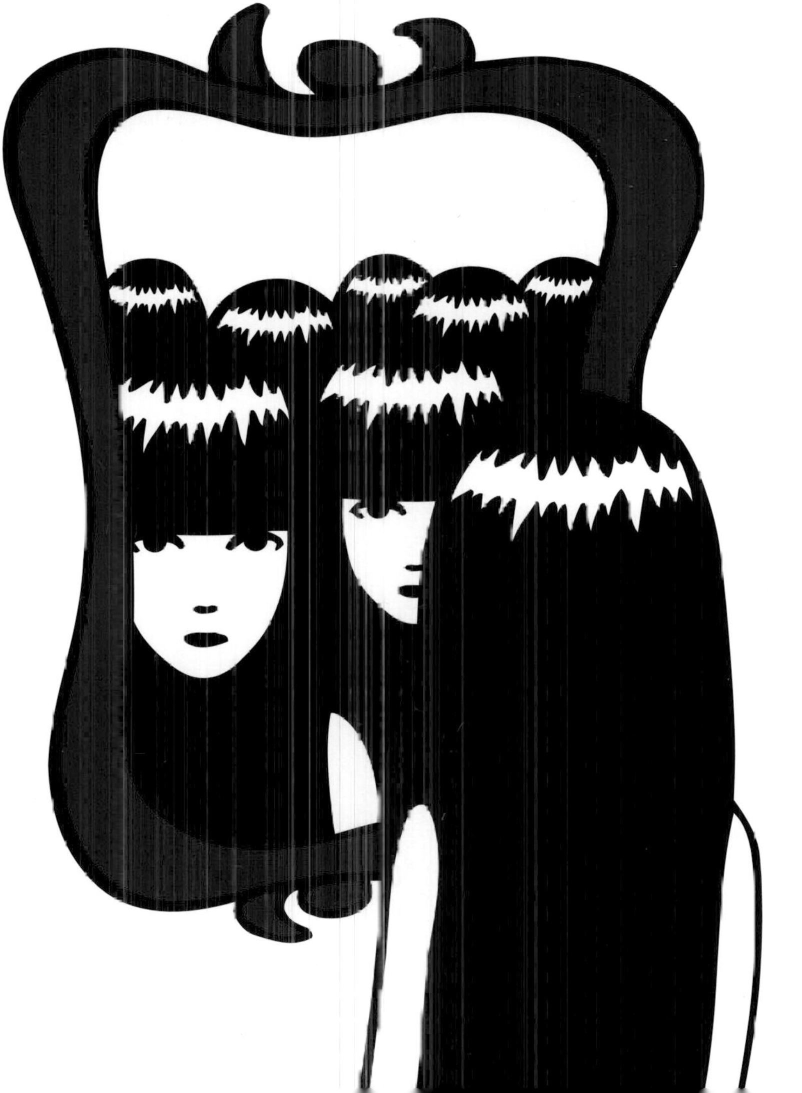

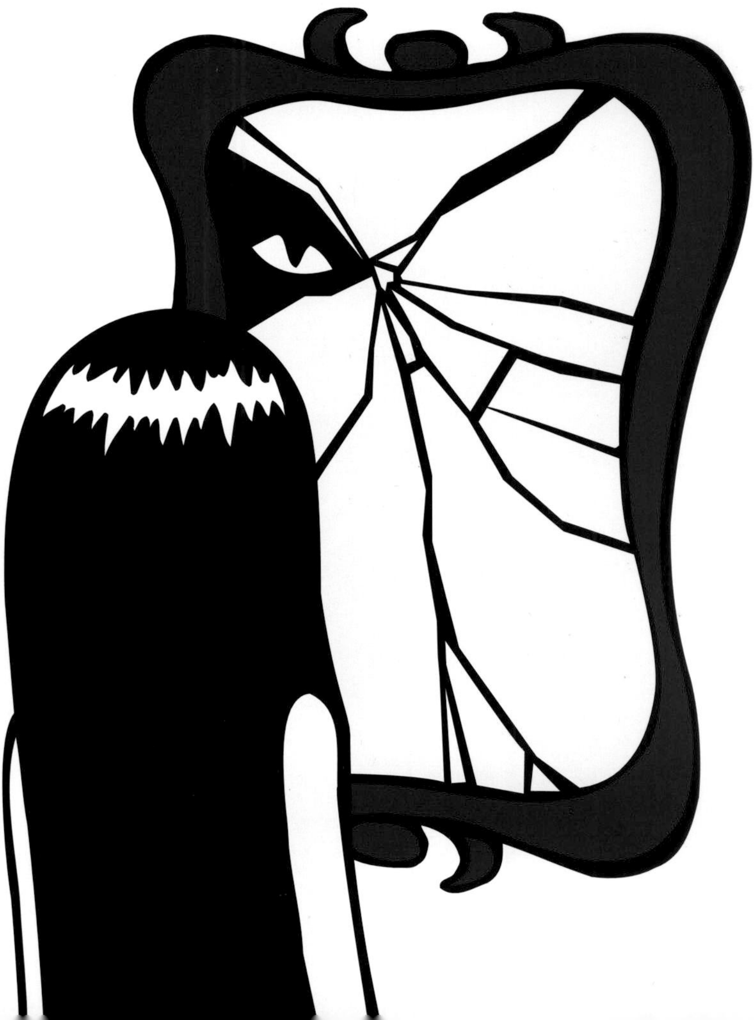

...seeing is deceiving.

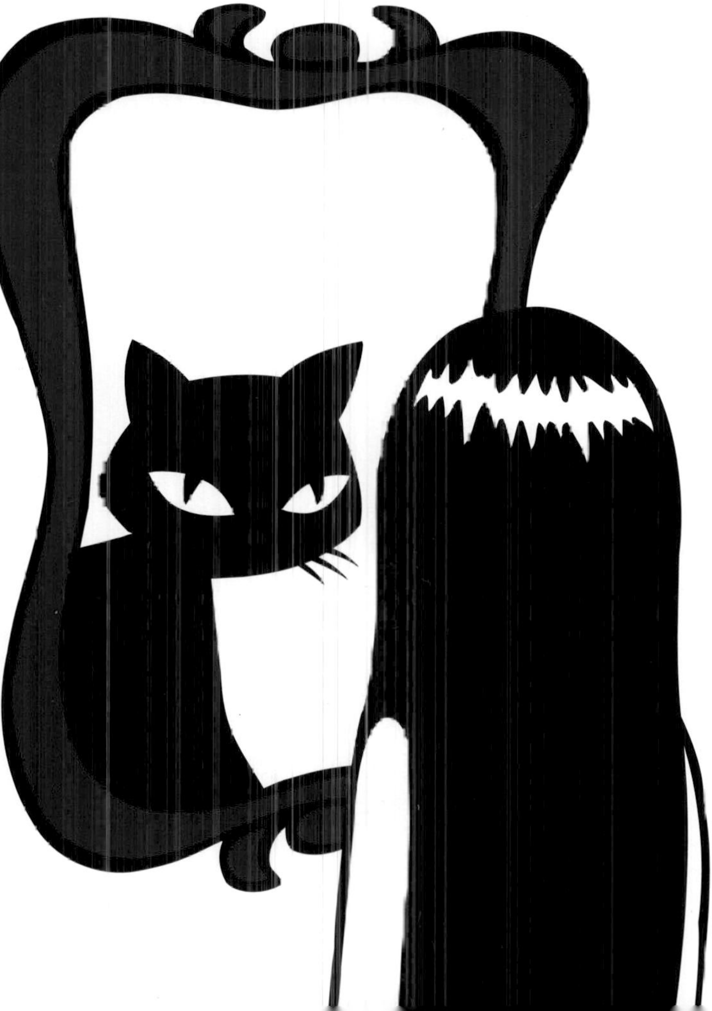

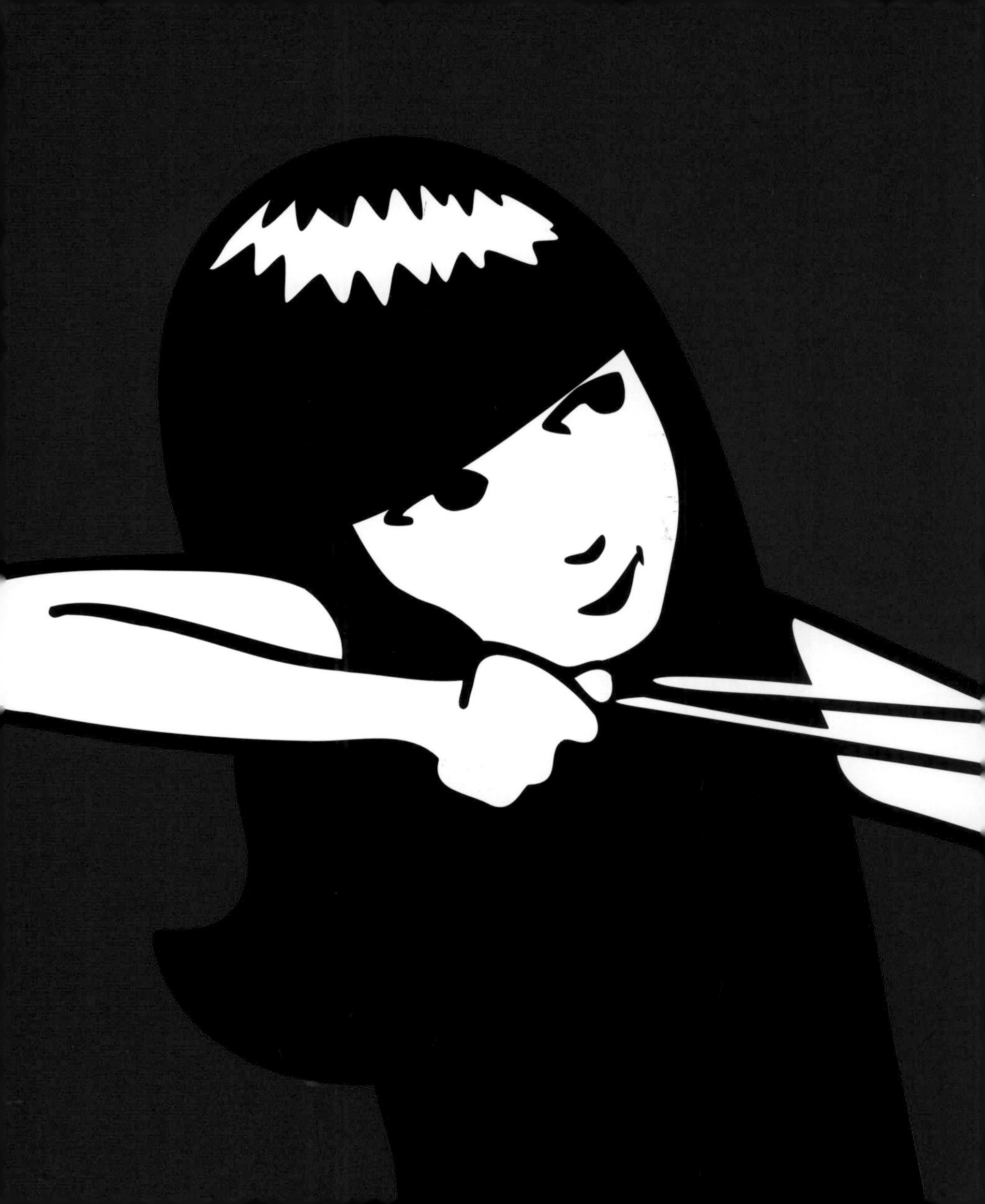

Emily doesn't aim high ...

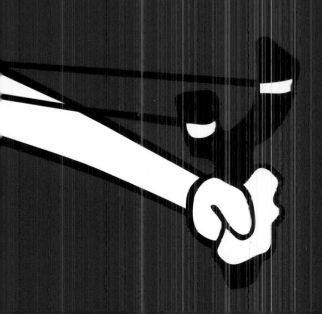

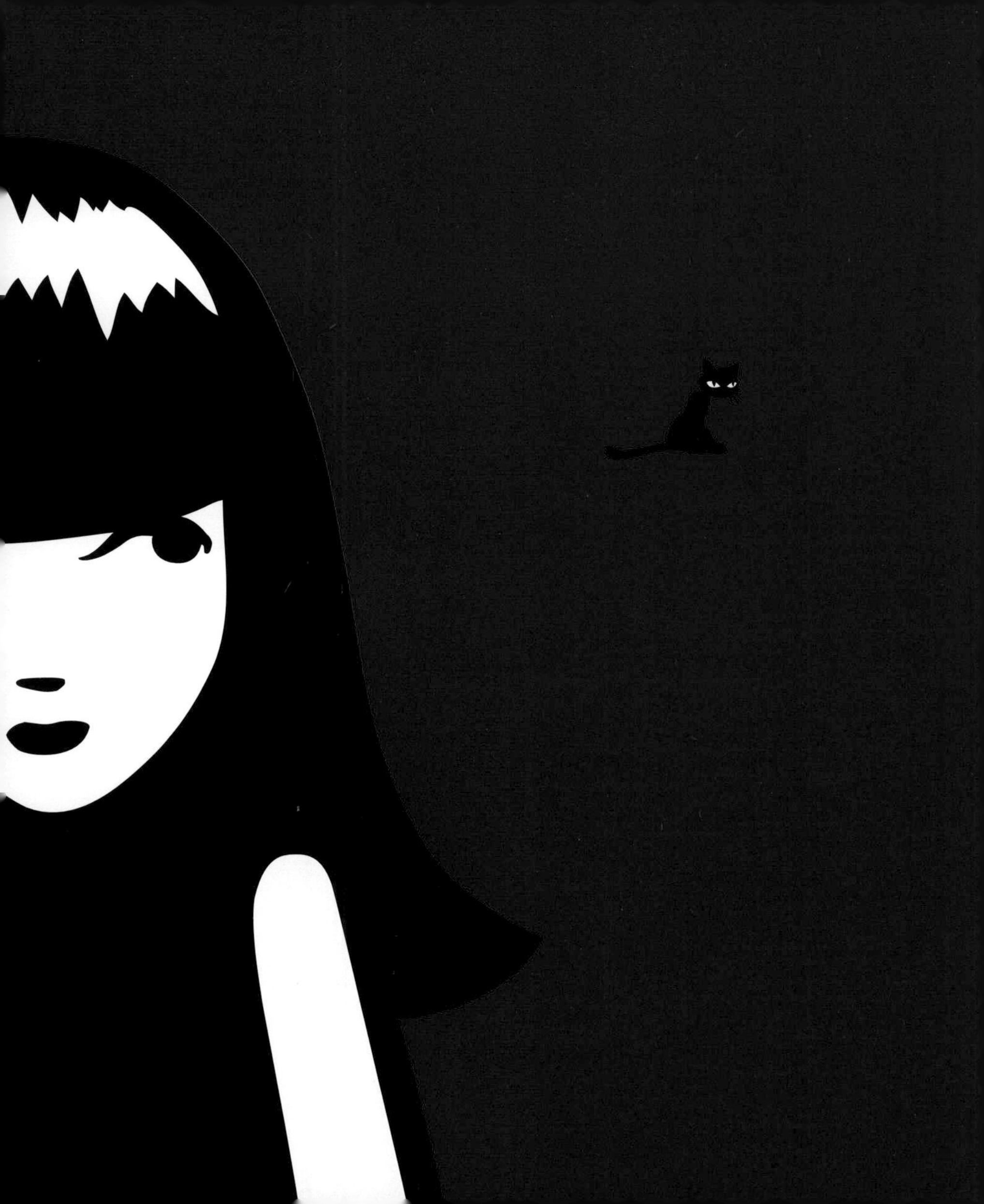

...she aims low.

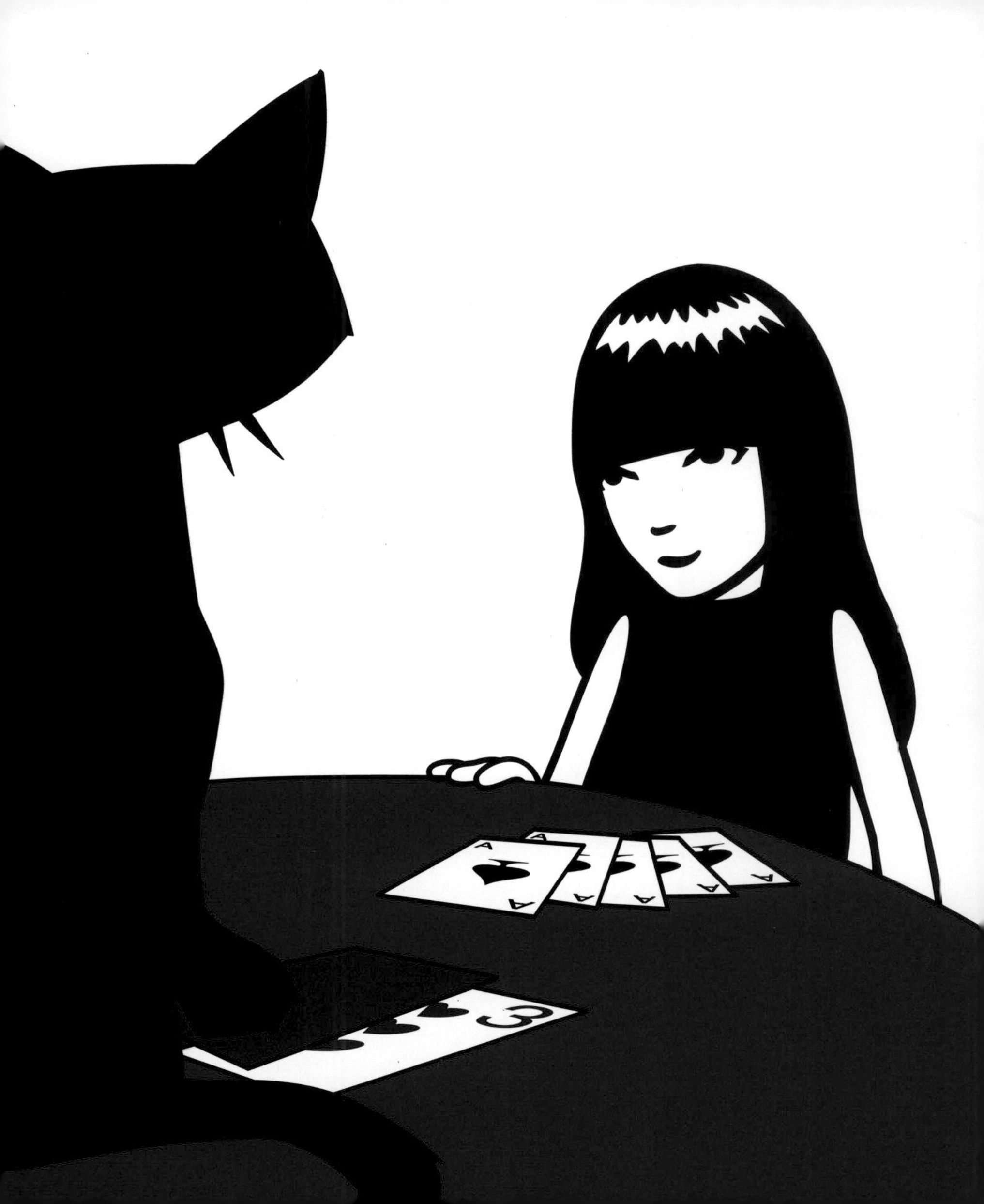

Emily doesn't cheat...

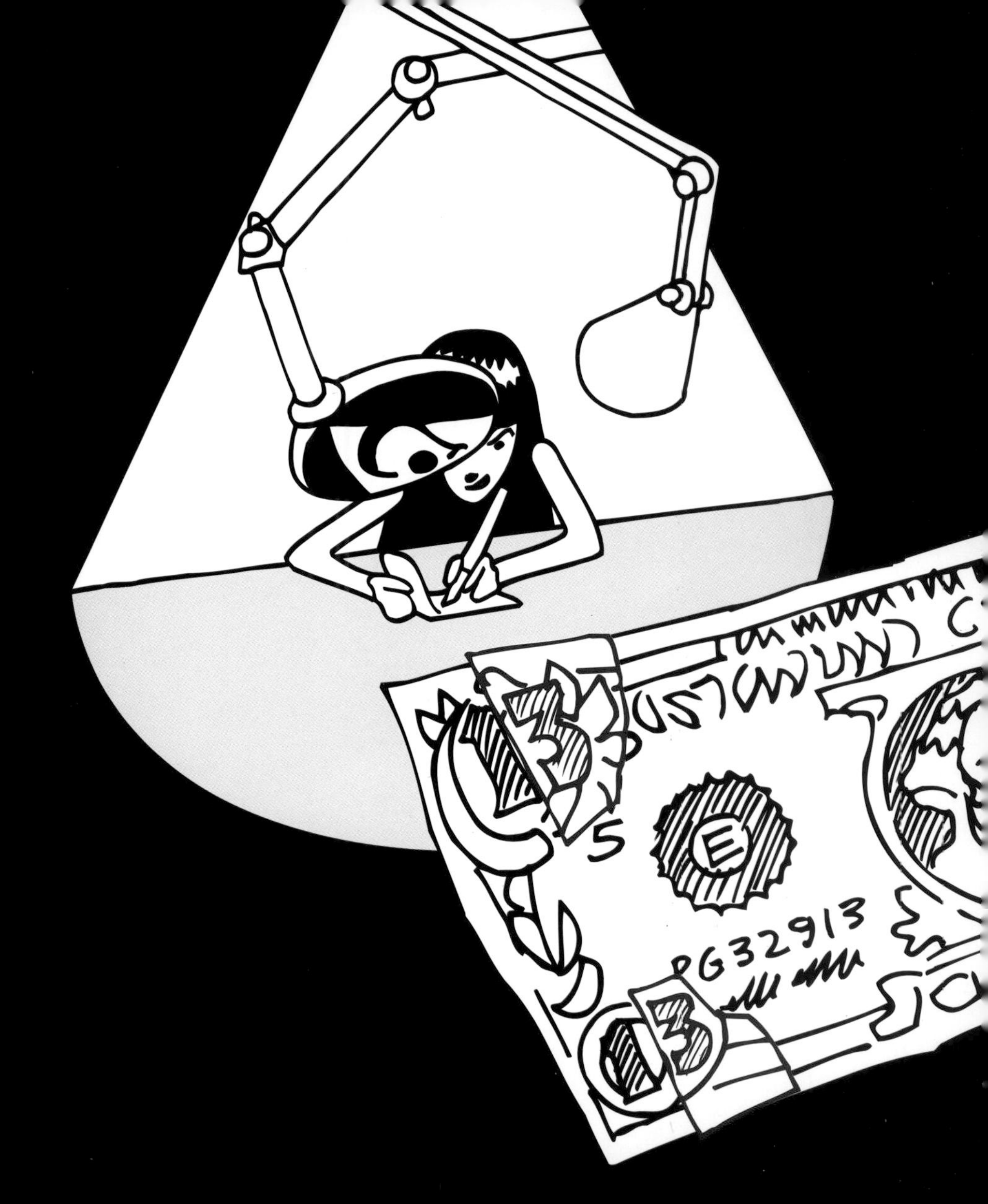
PG32913

...she plays by her own rules.

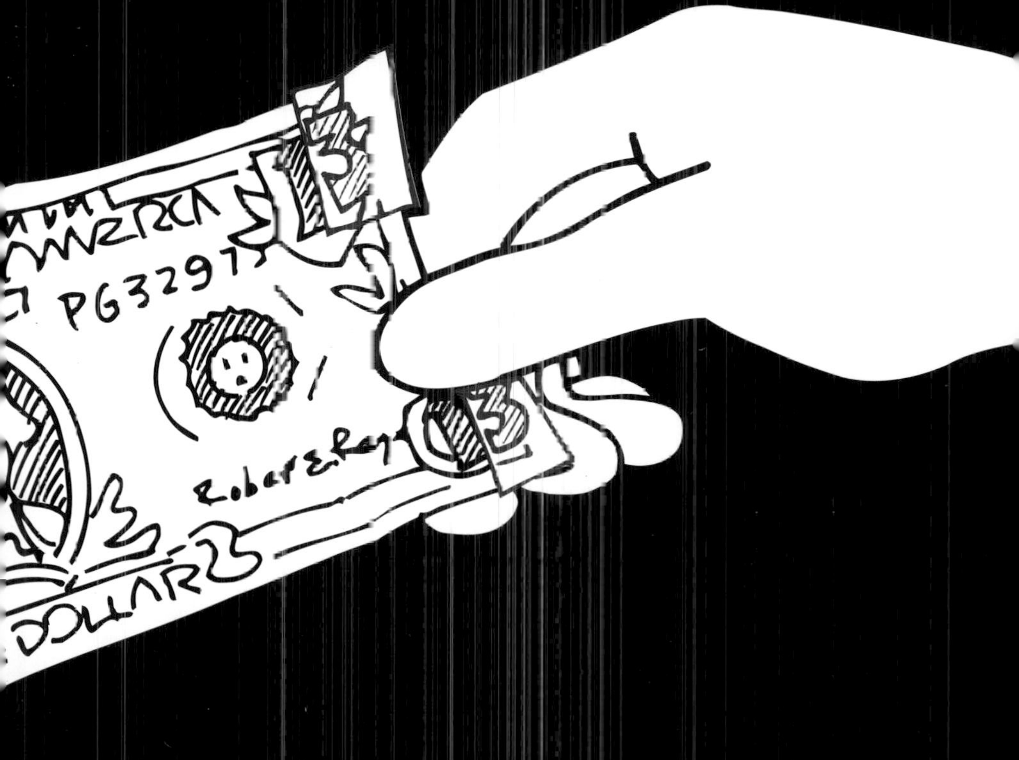

Emily doesn't just break rules...

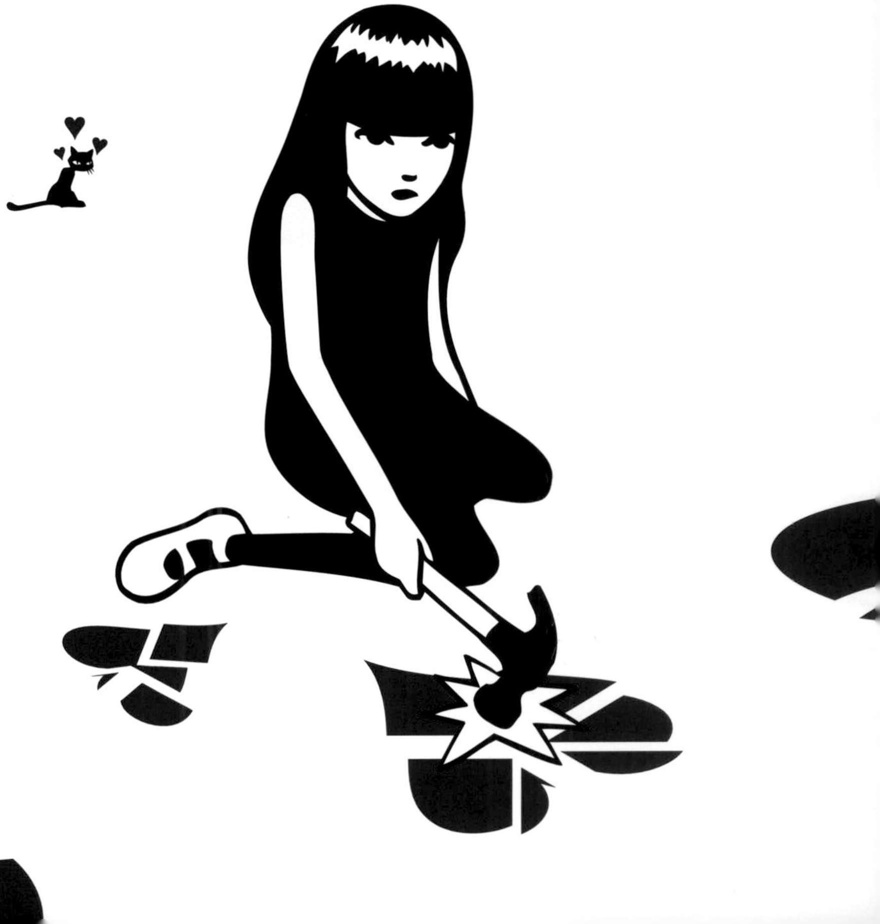

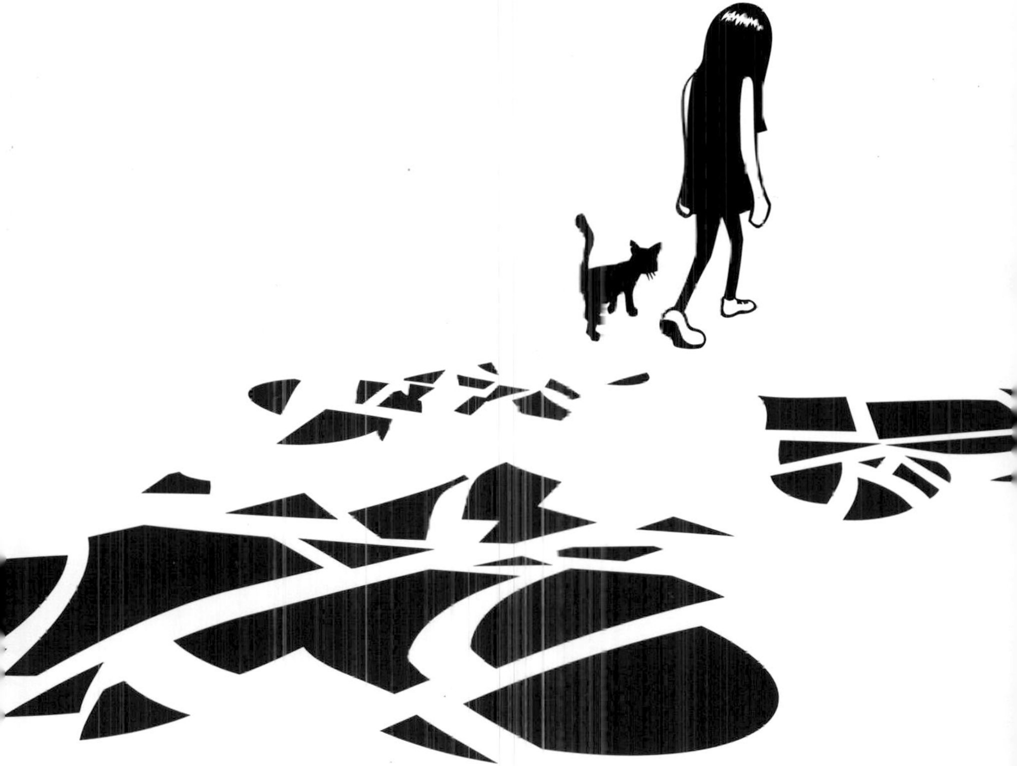

...she breaks hearts.

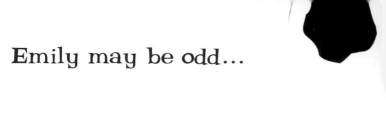

Emily may be odd...

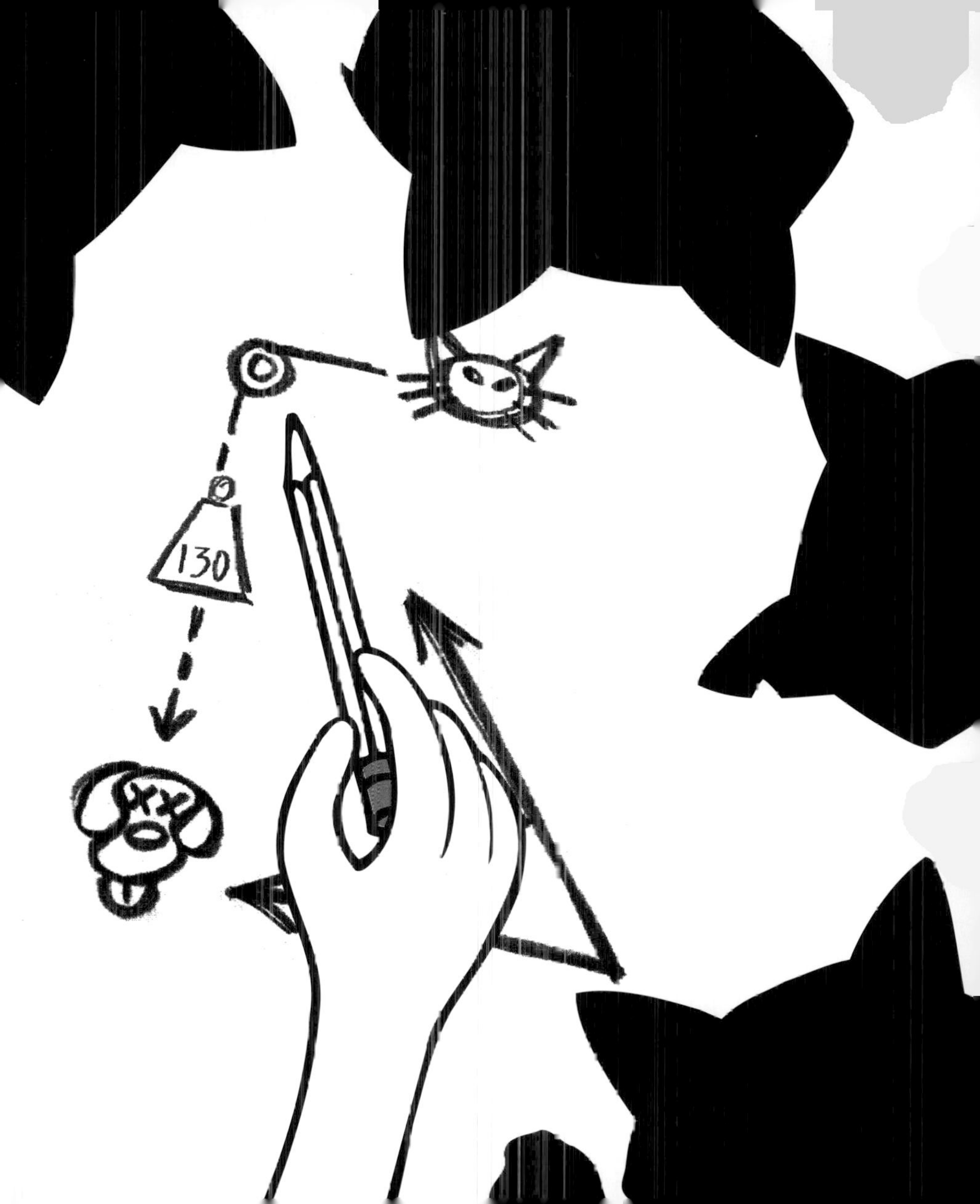
130

...but she always gets even.

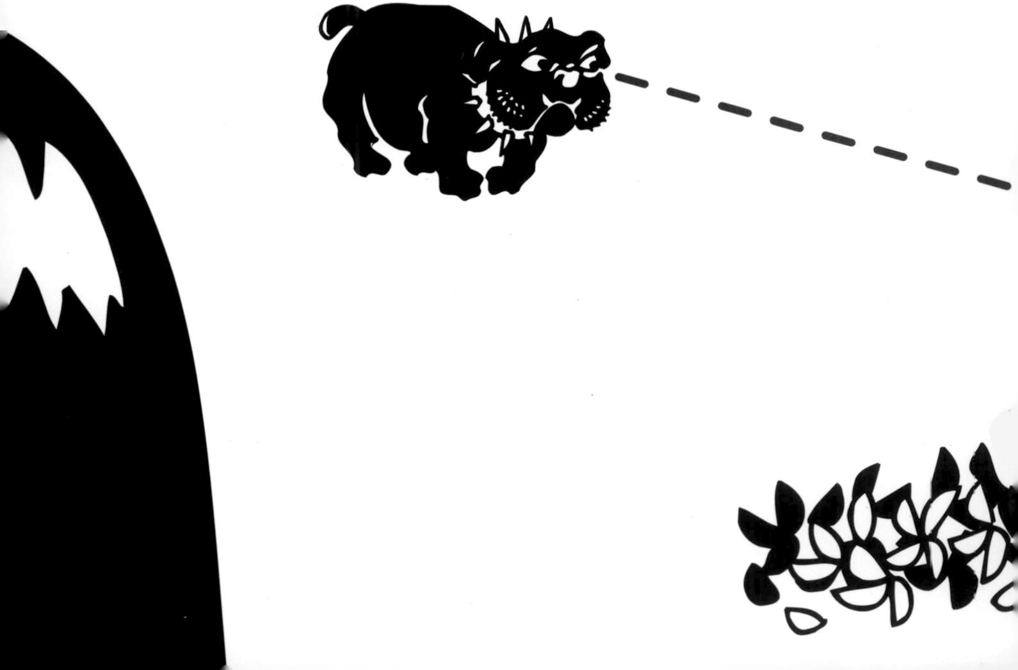

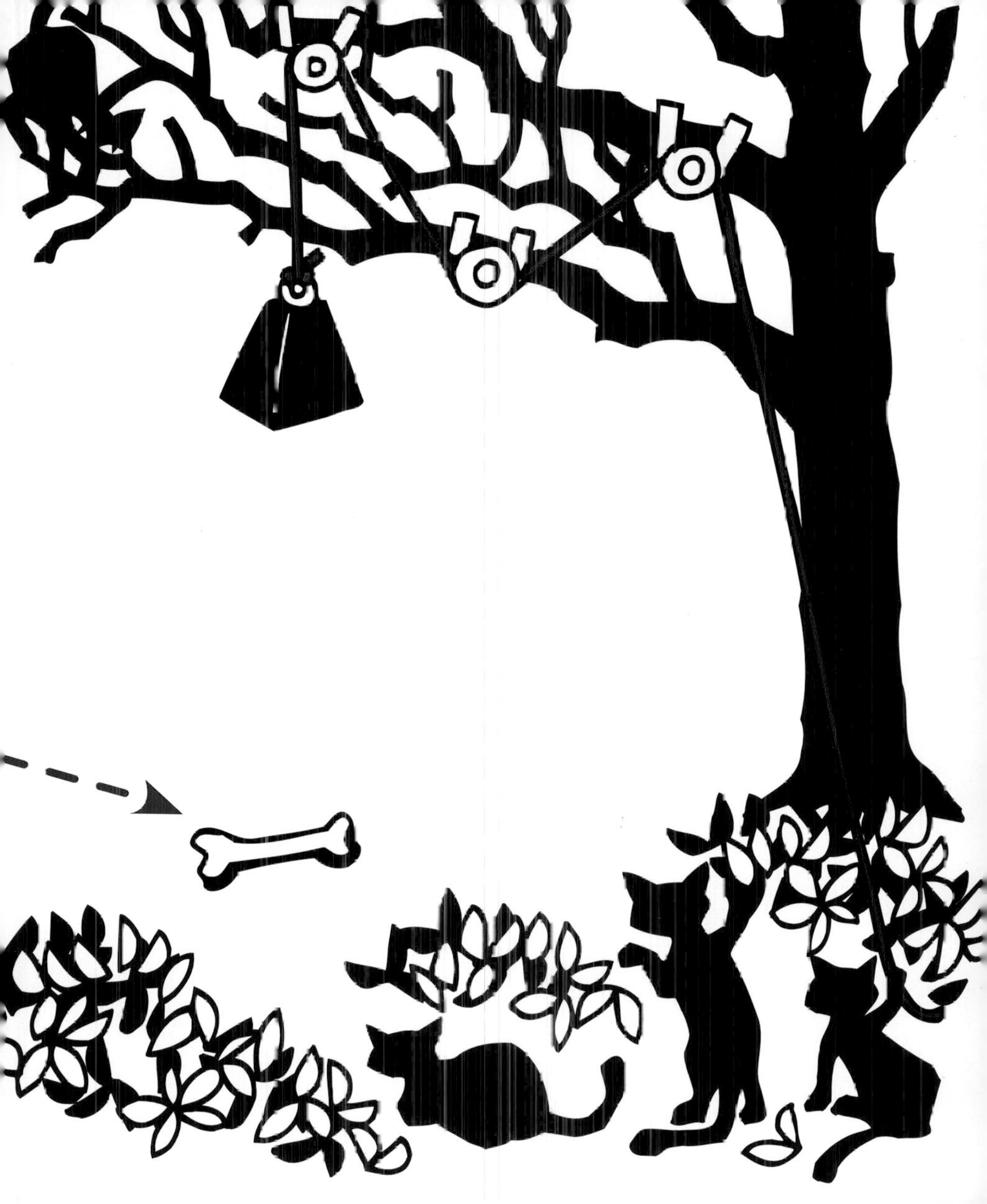

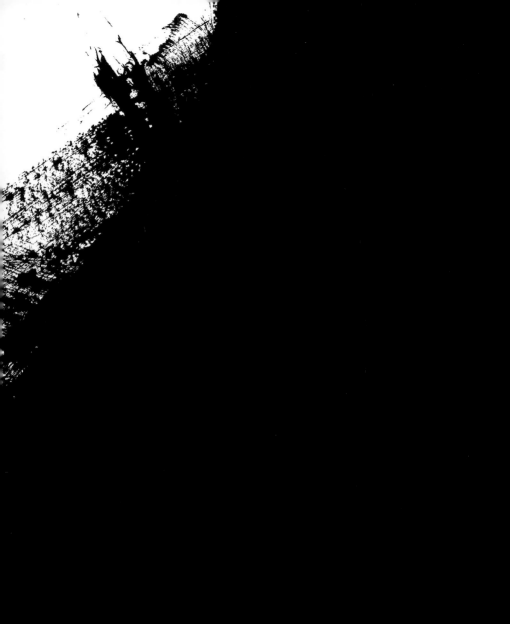

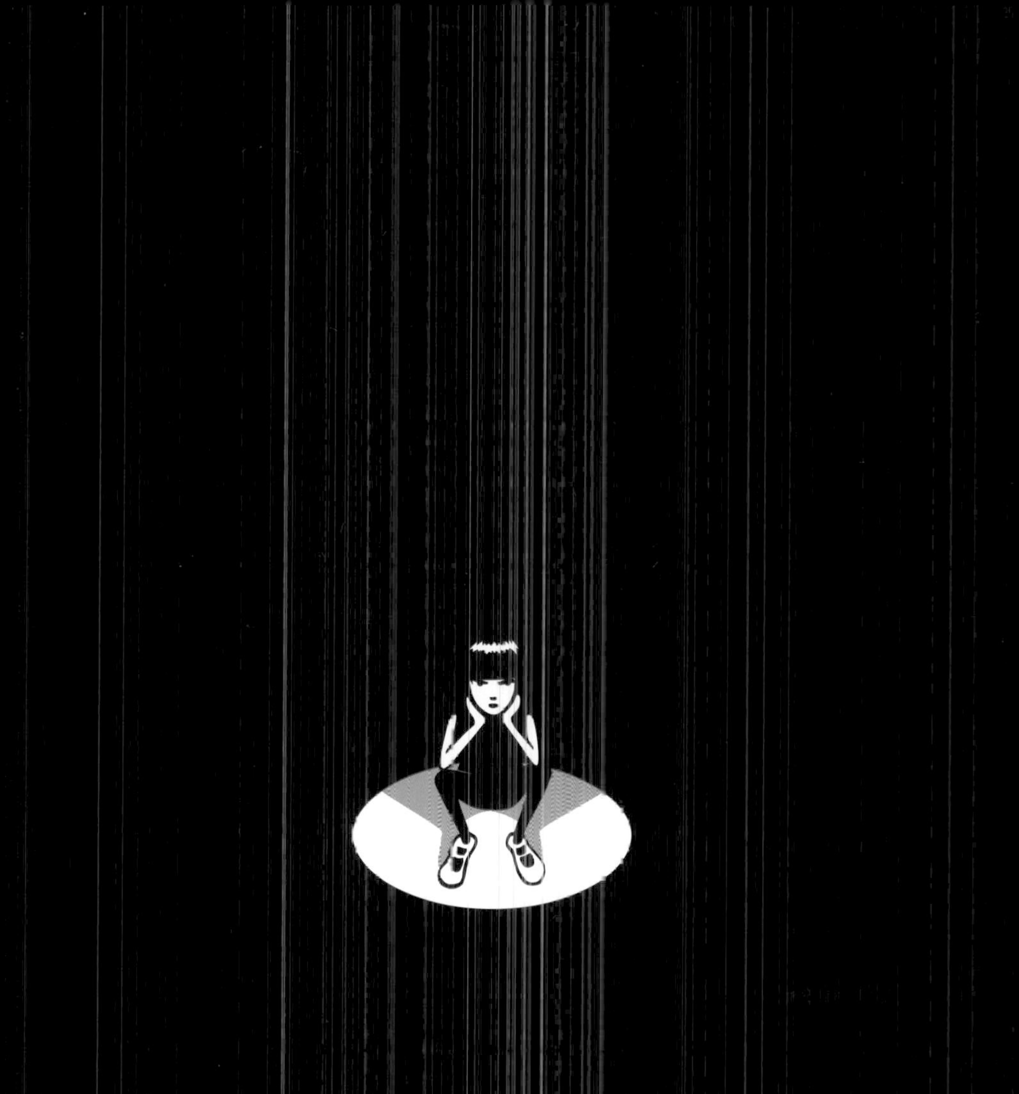

Emily doesn't make imaginary friends…

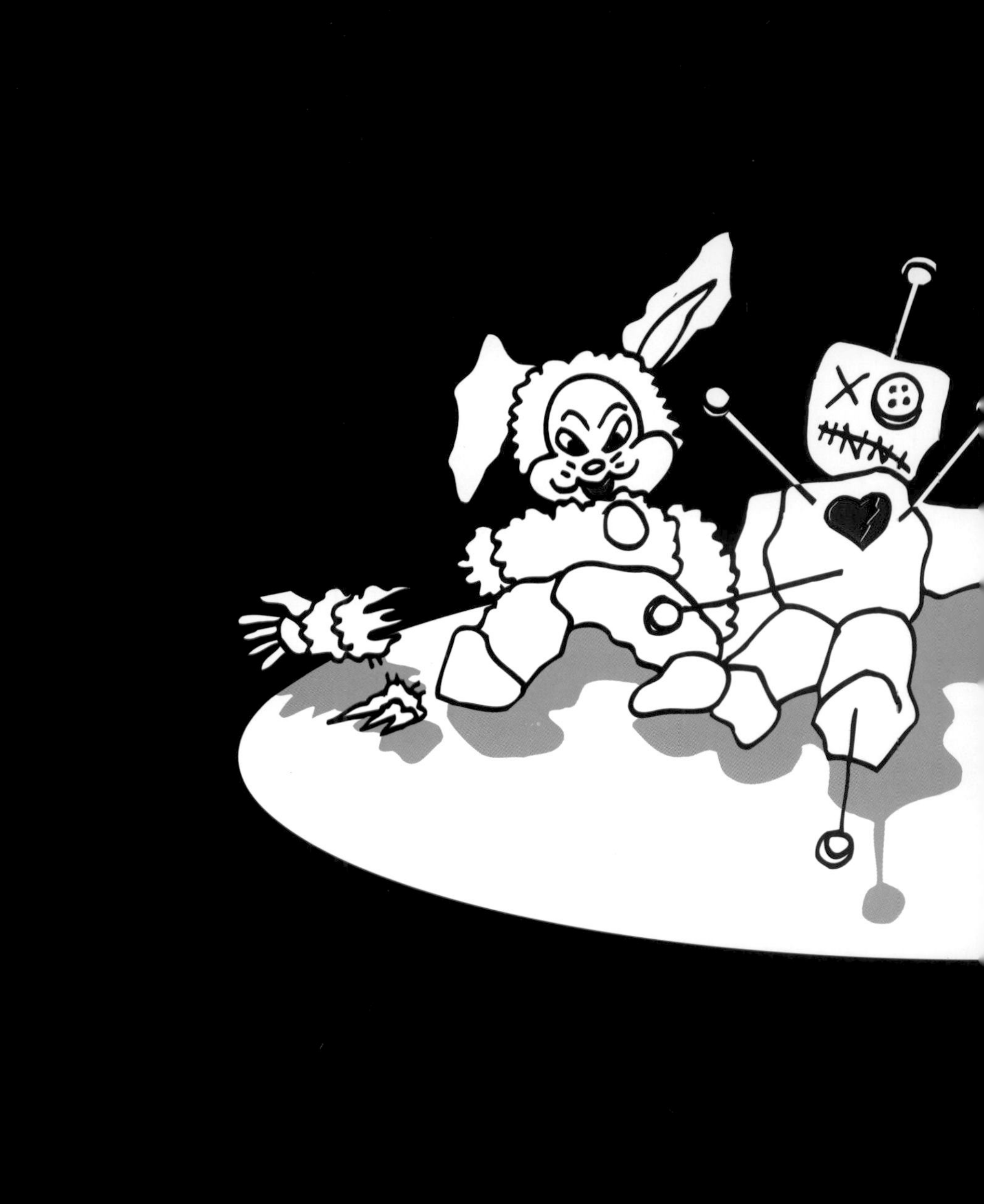

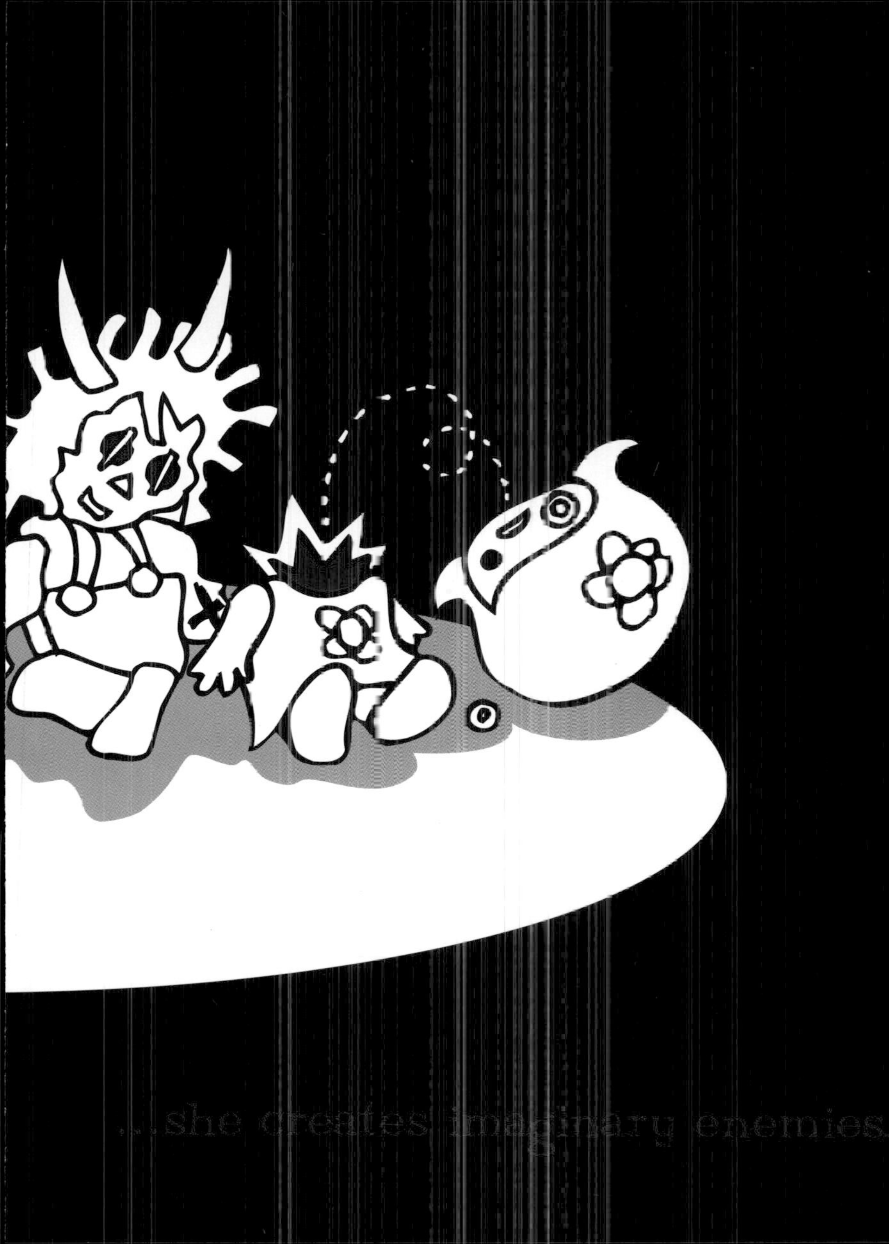

...she creates imaginary enemies.

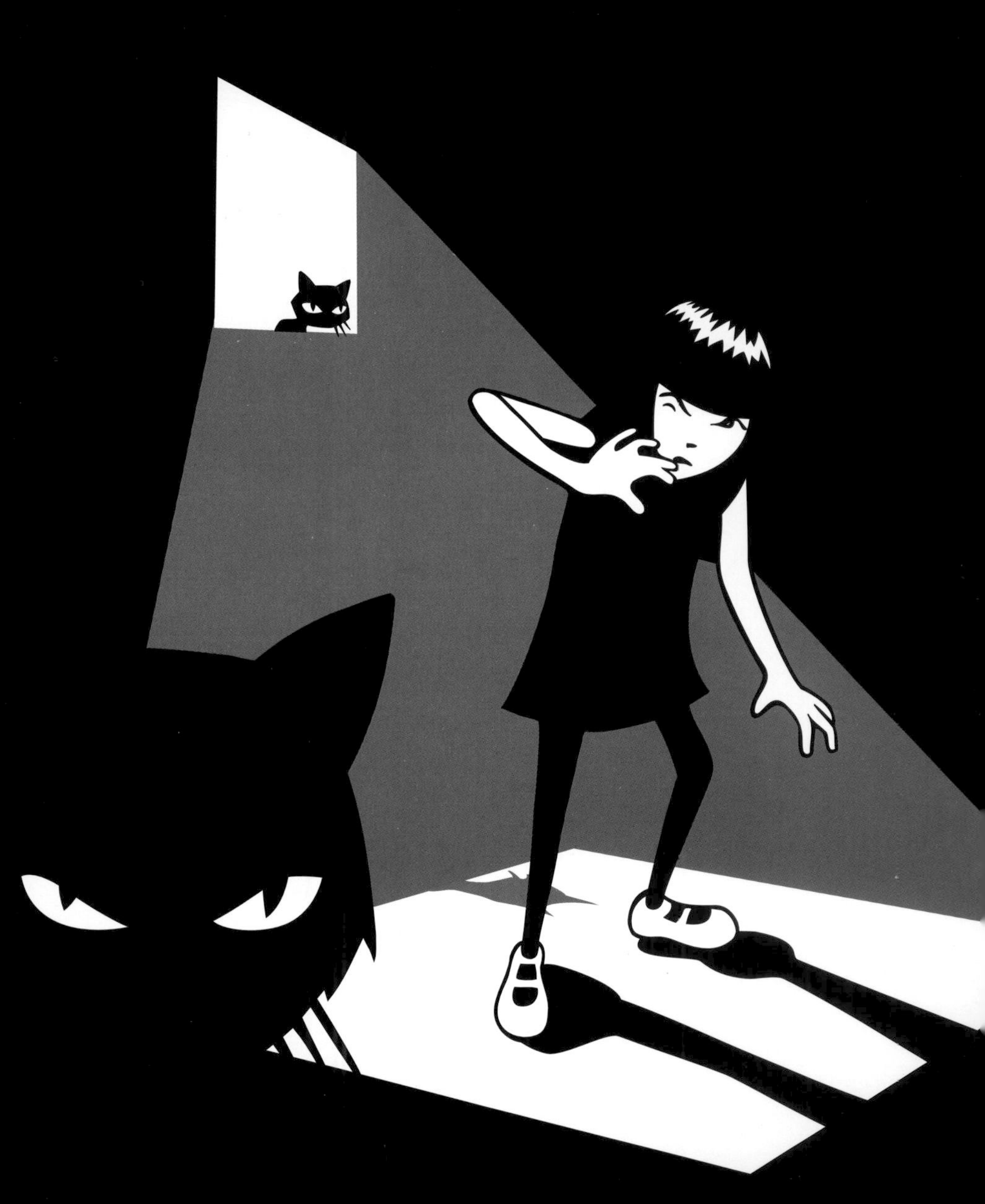

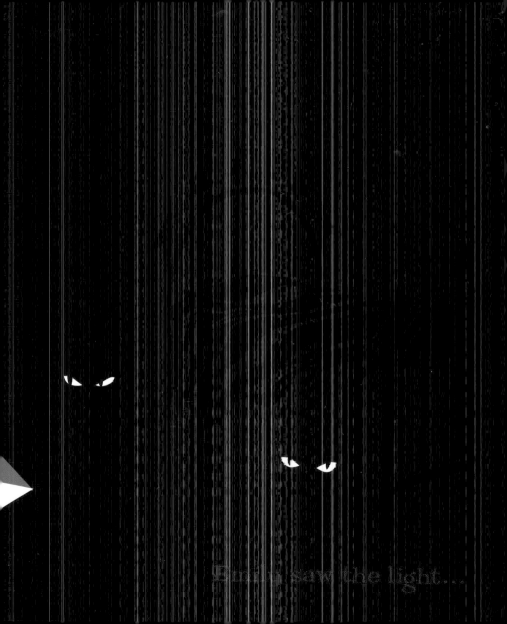

Emily saw the light...

…and she wasn't impressed.

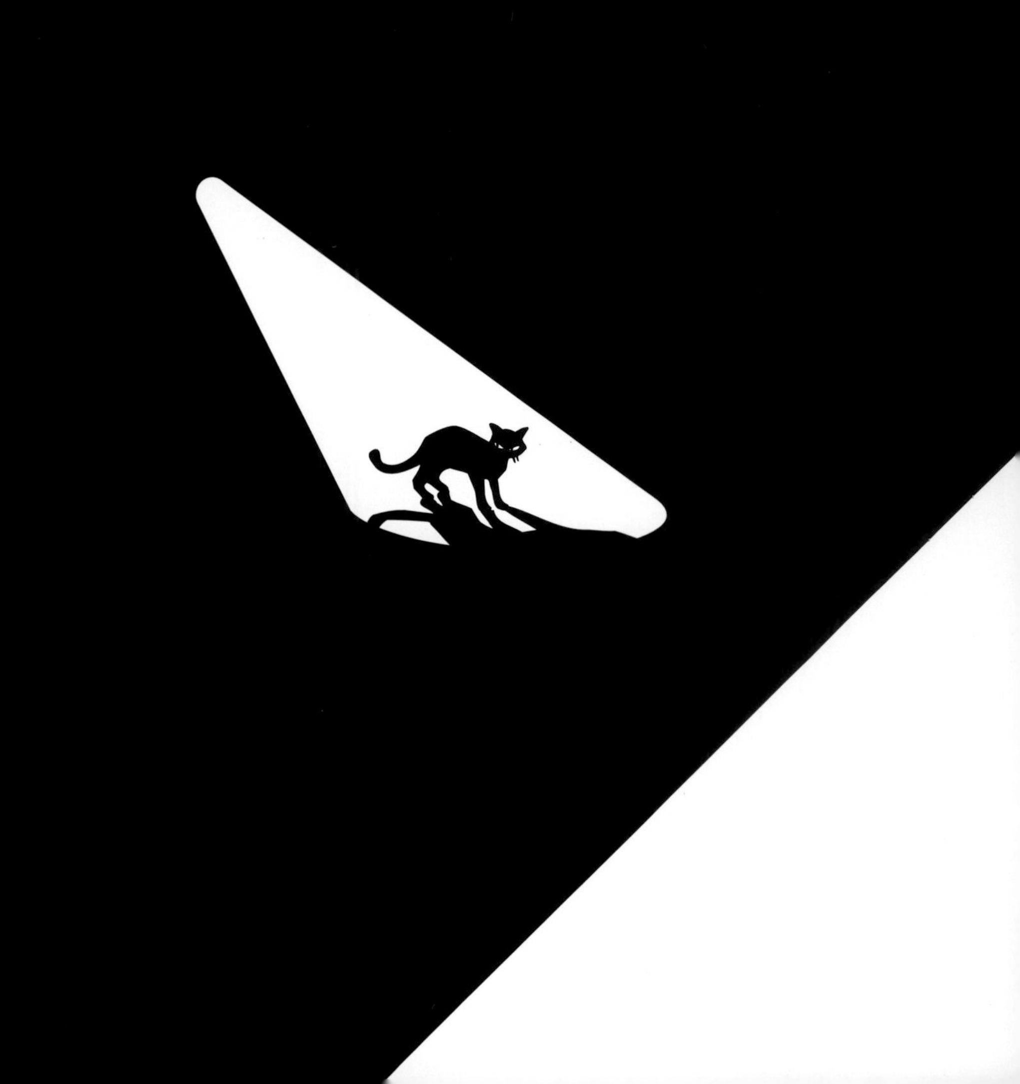

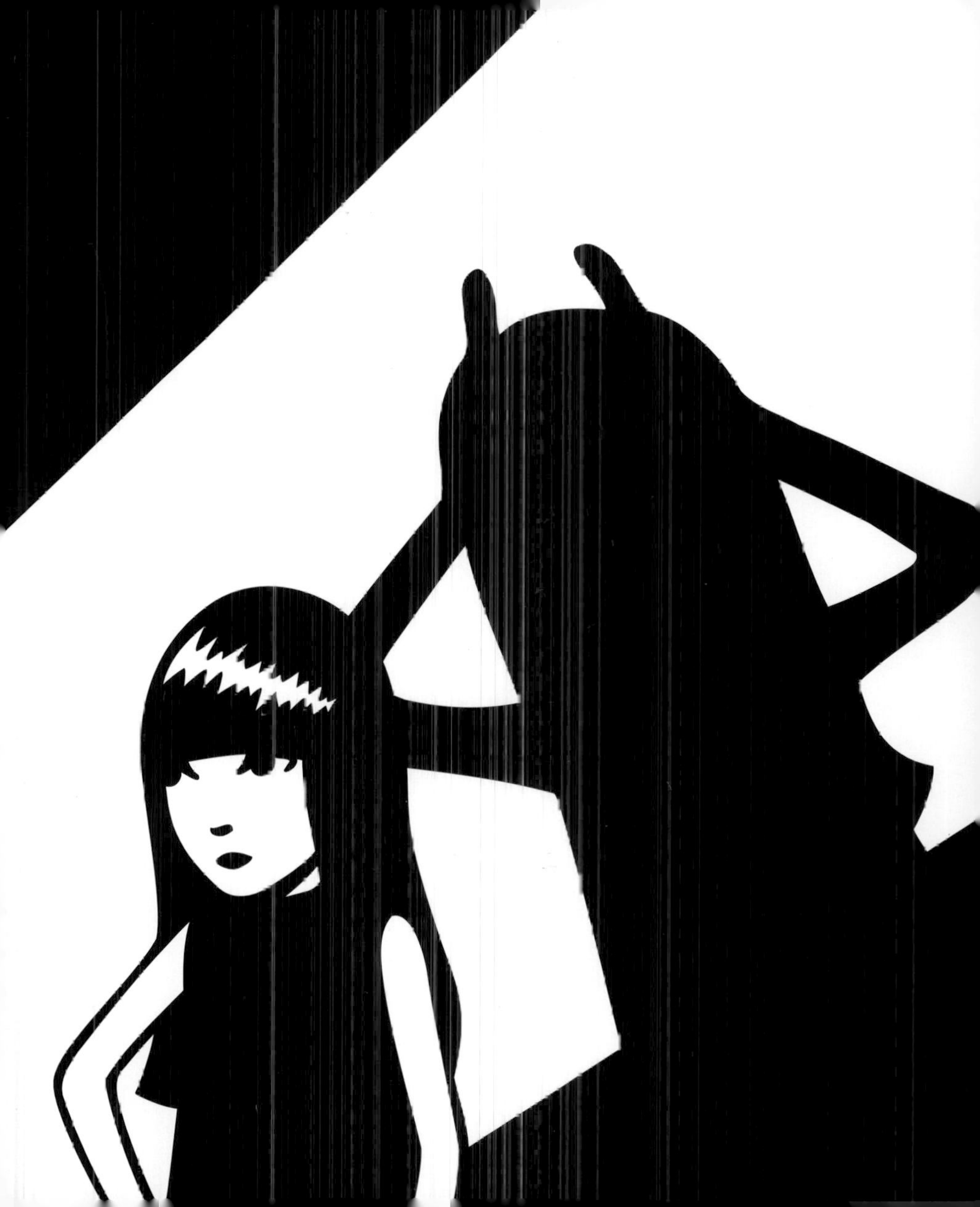

Emily isn't crazy...

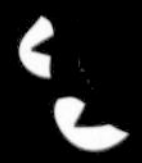

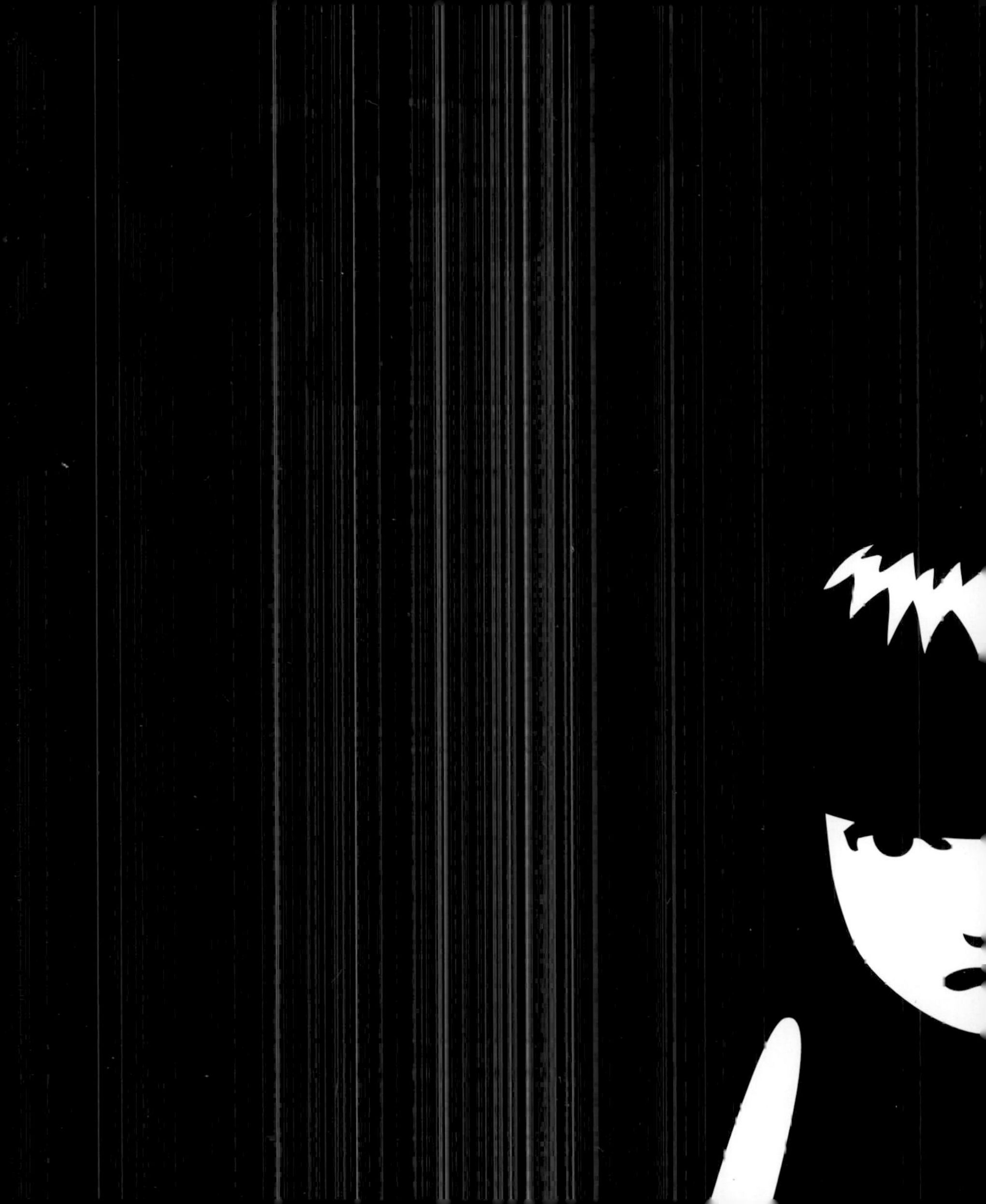

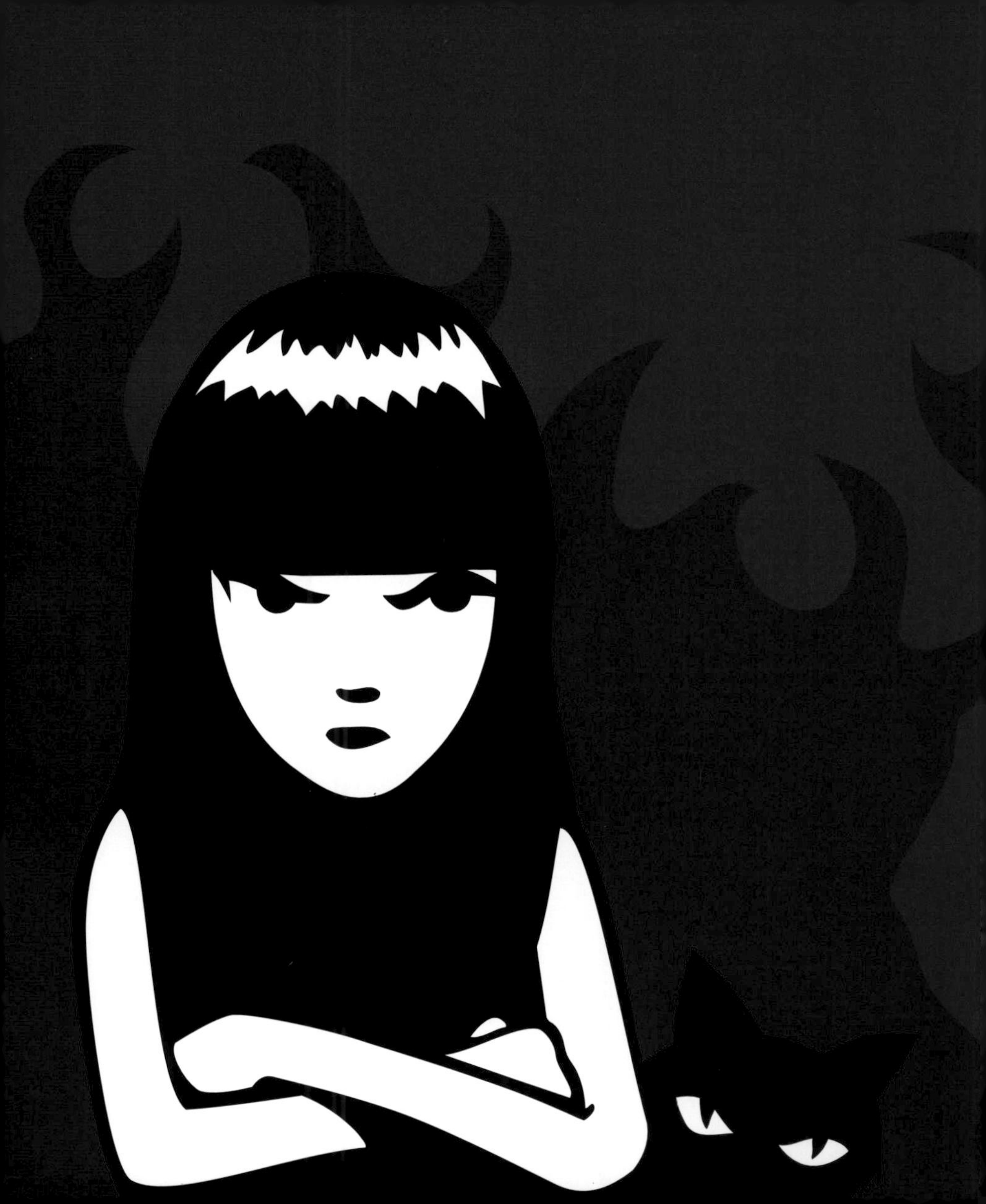

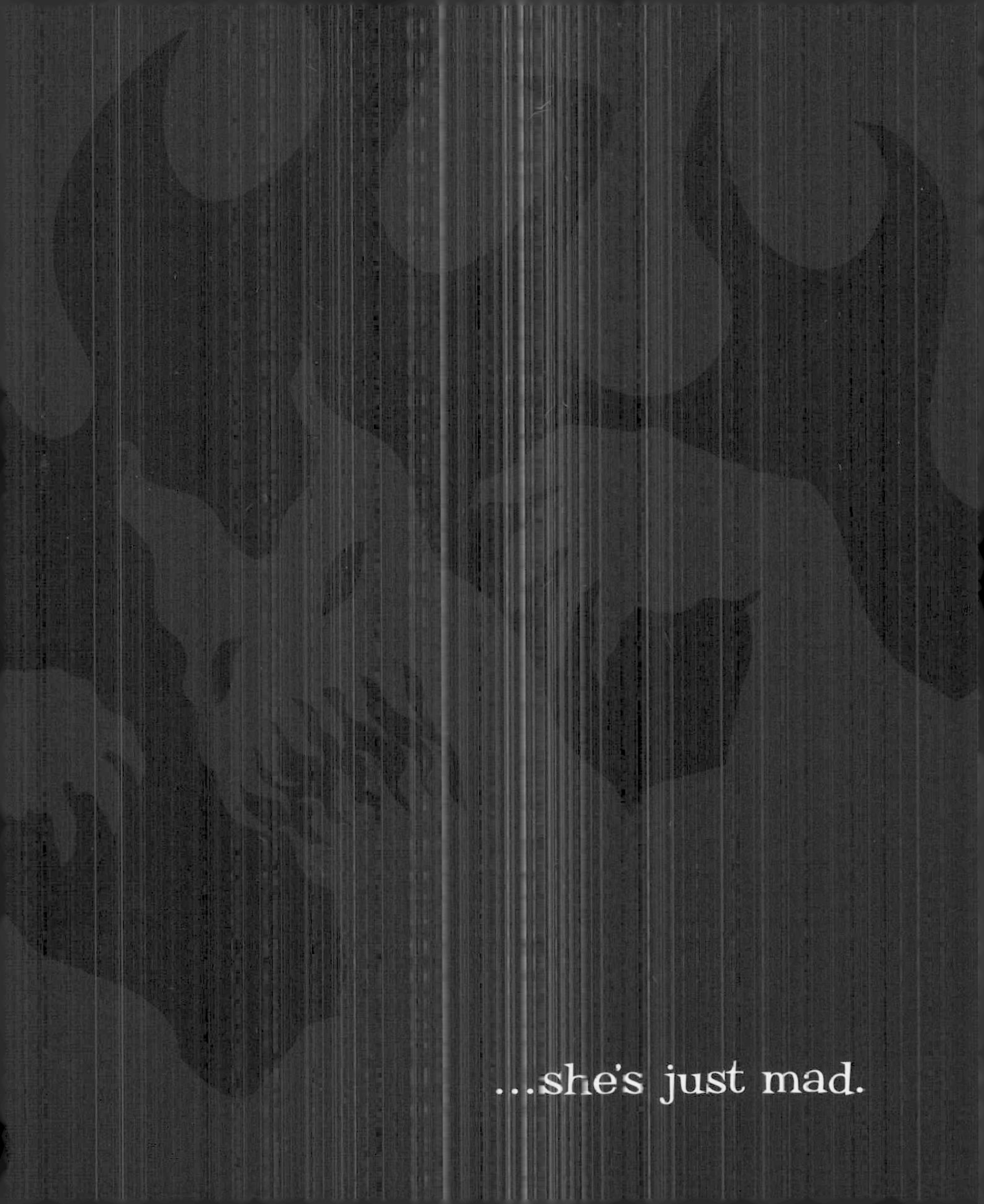

...she's just mad.

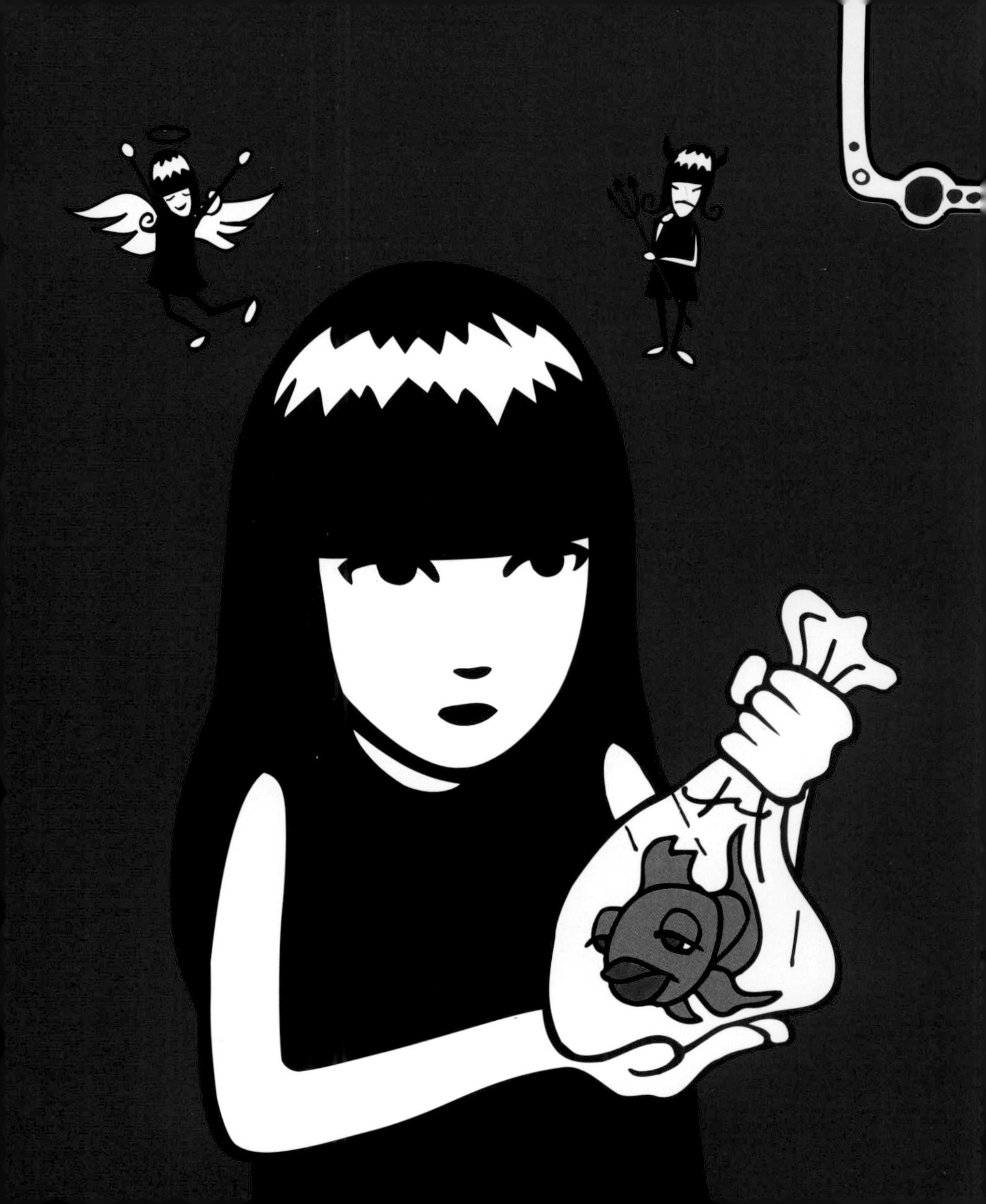

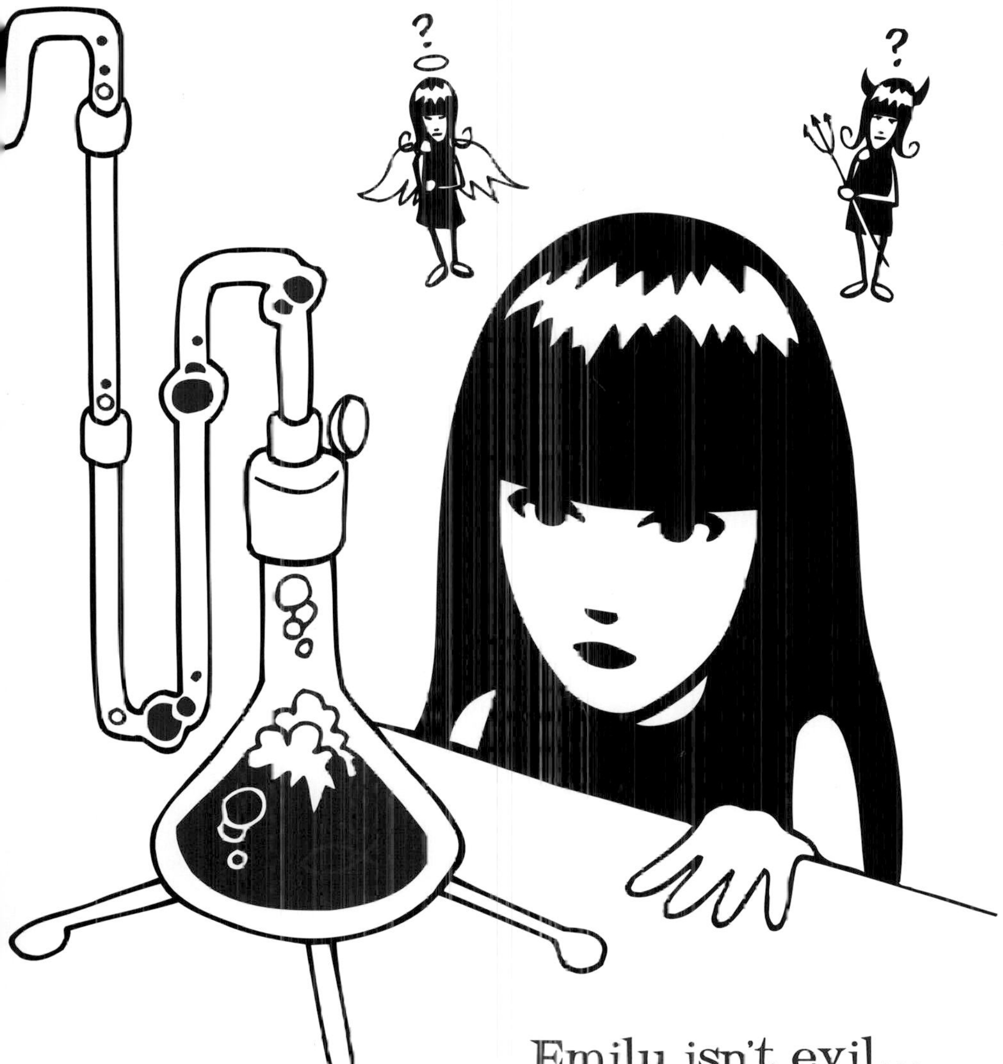
?
?

Emily isn't evil...

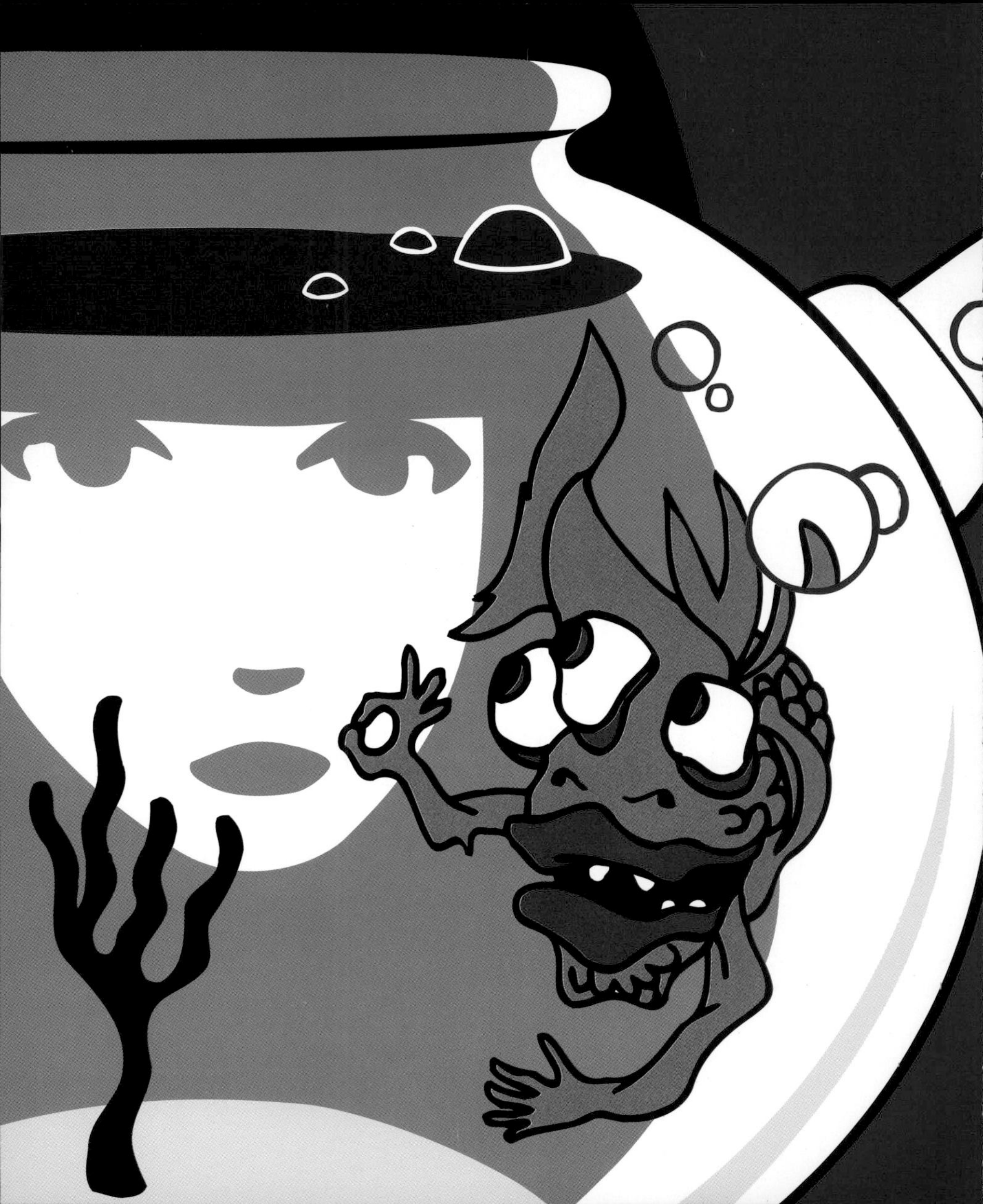

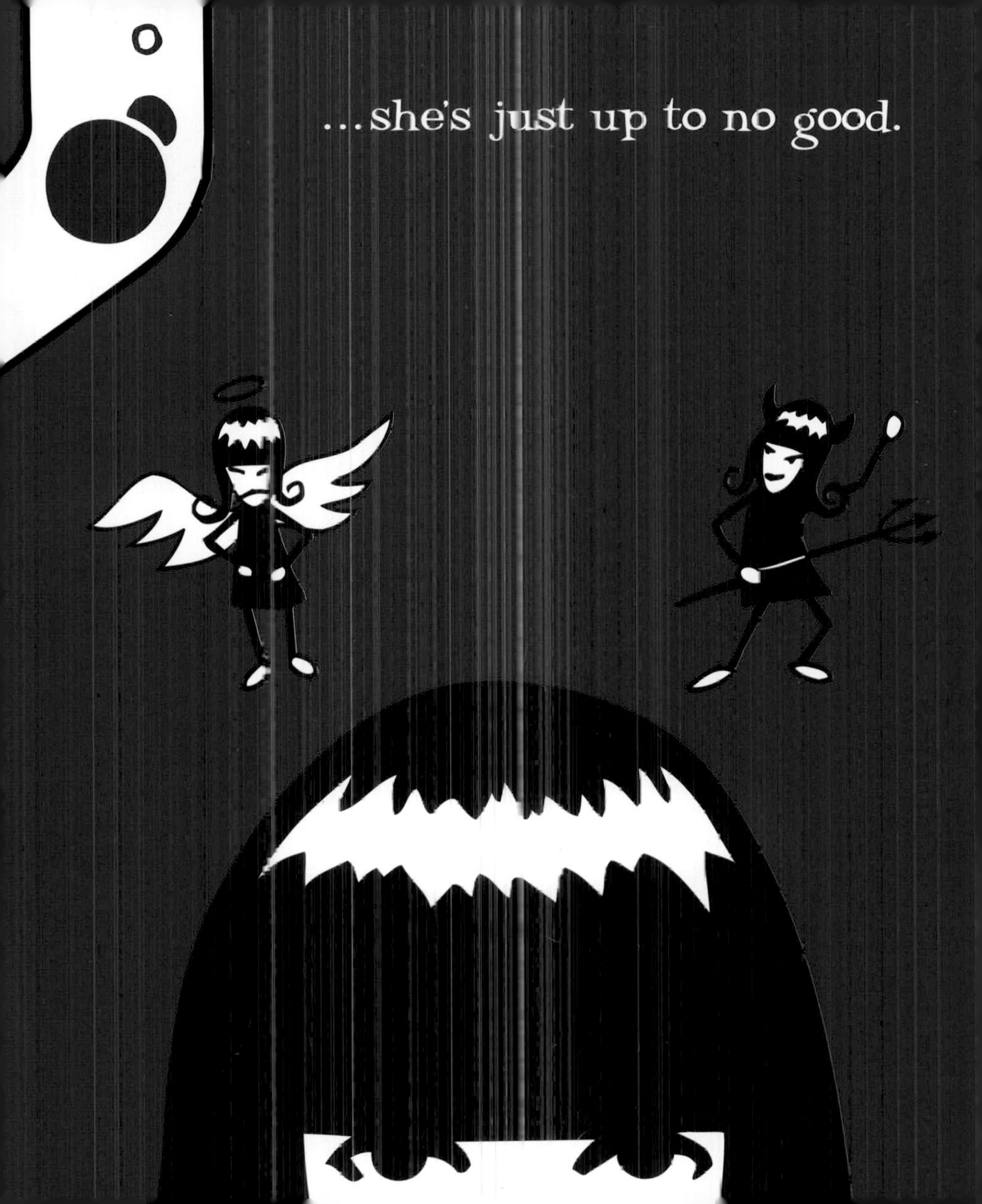
...she's just up to no good.

Emily's dream...

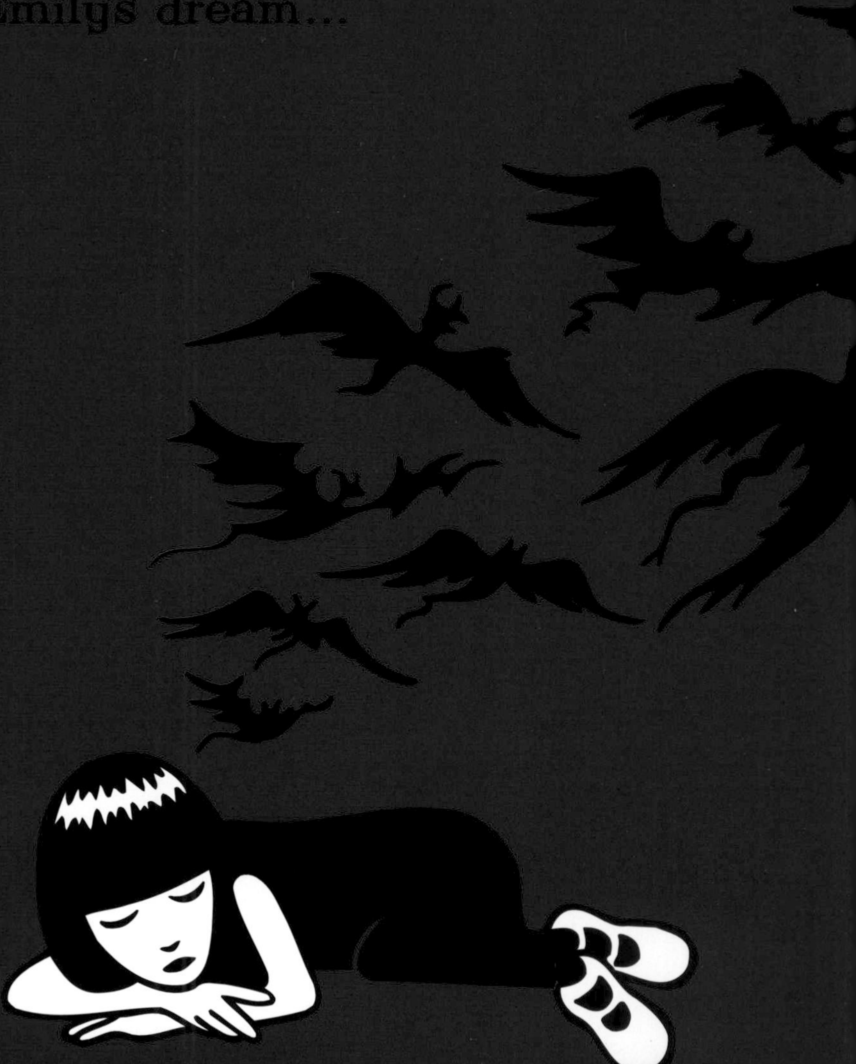

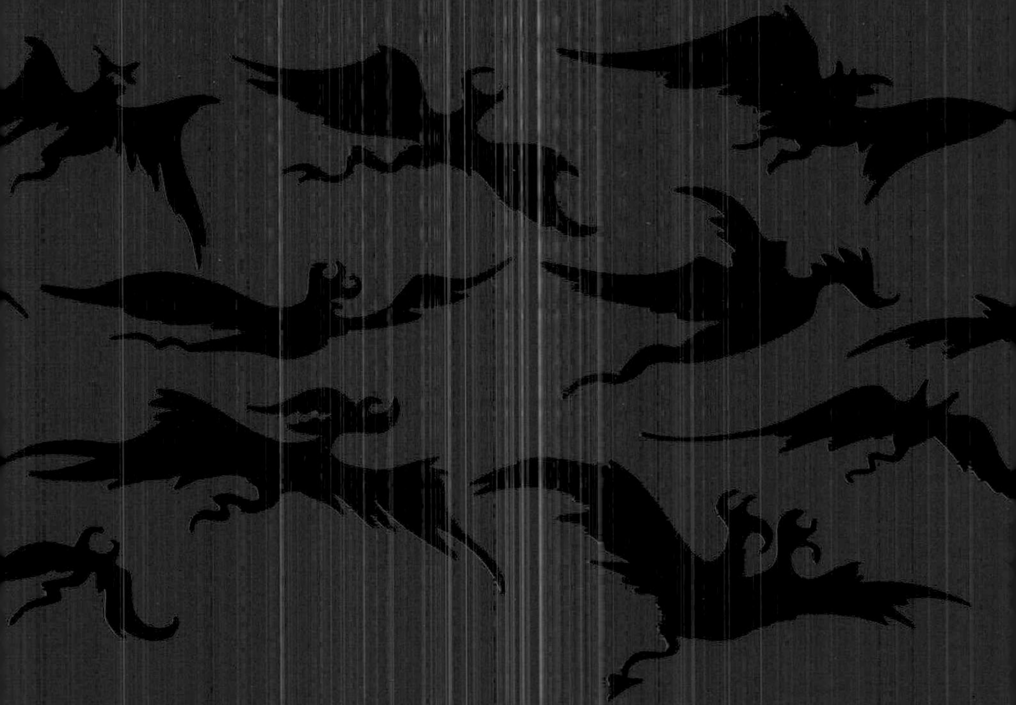

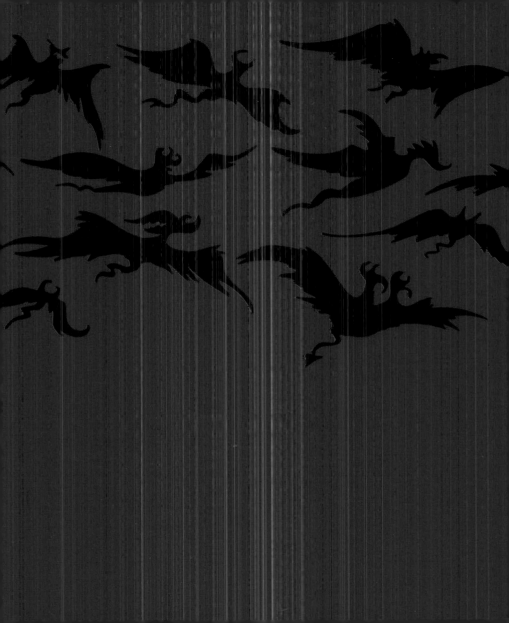

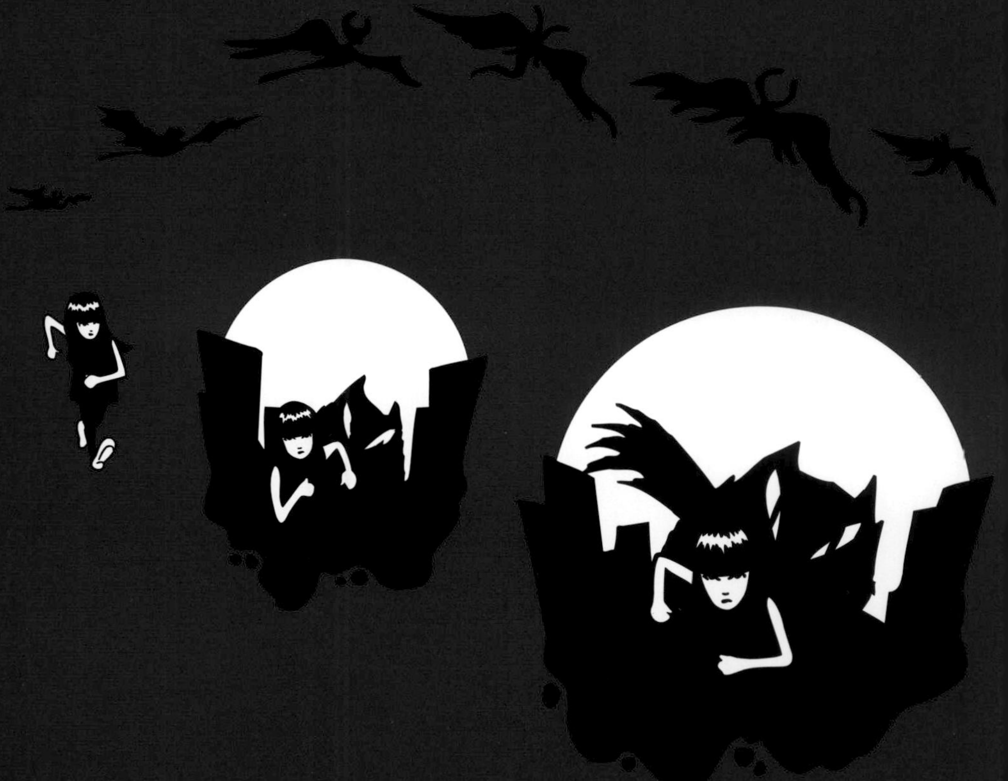

...is your worst nightmare.

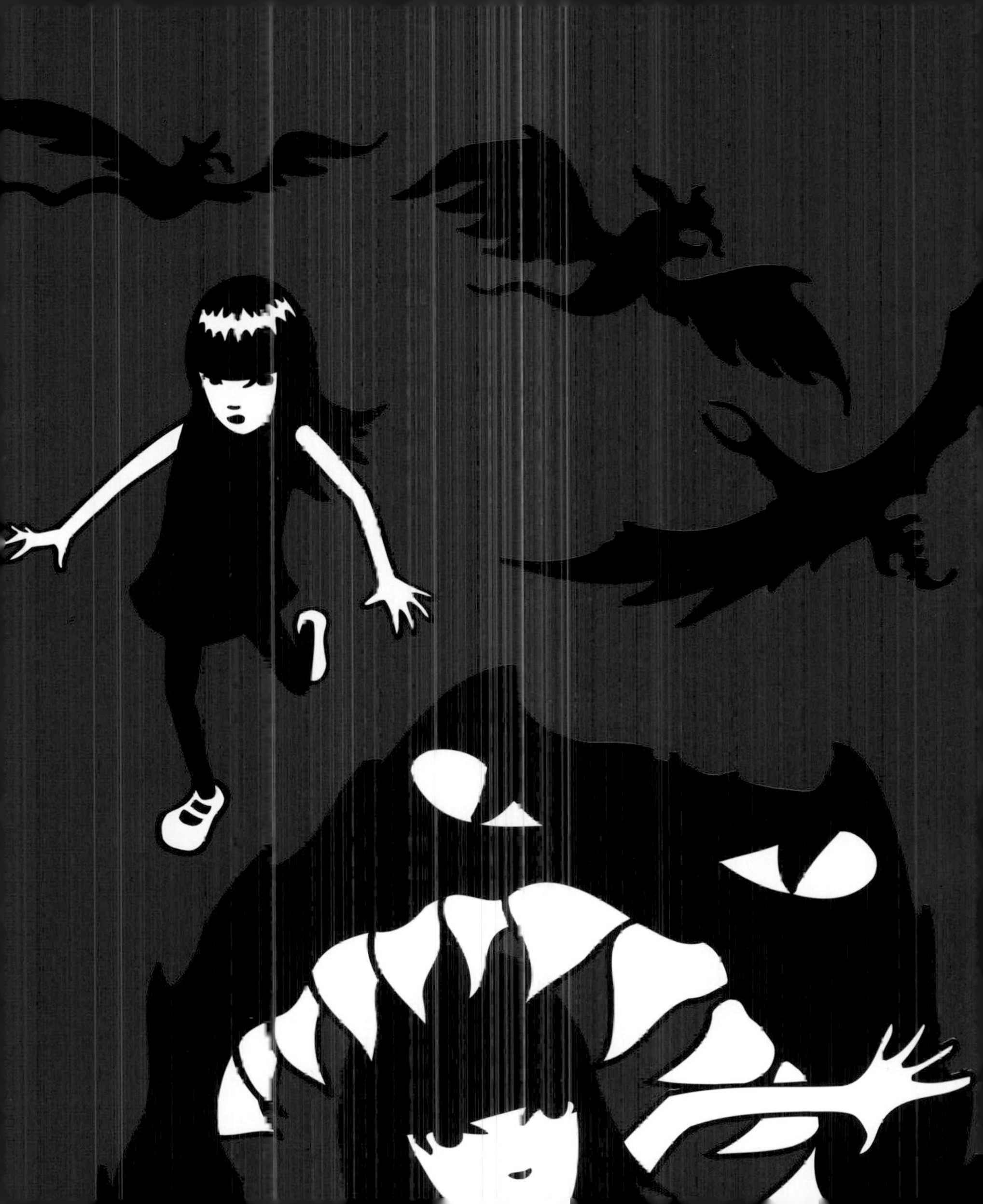

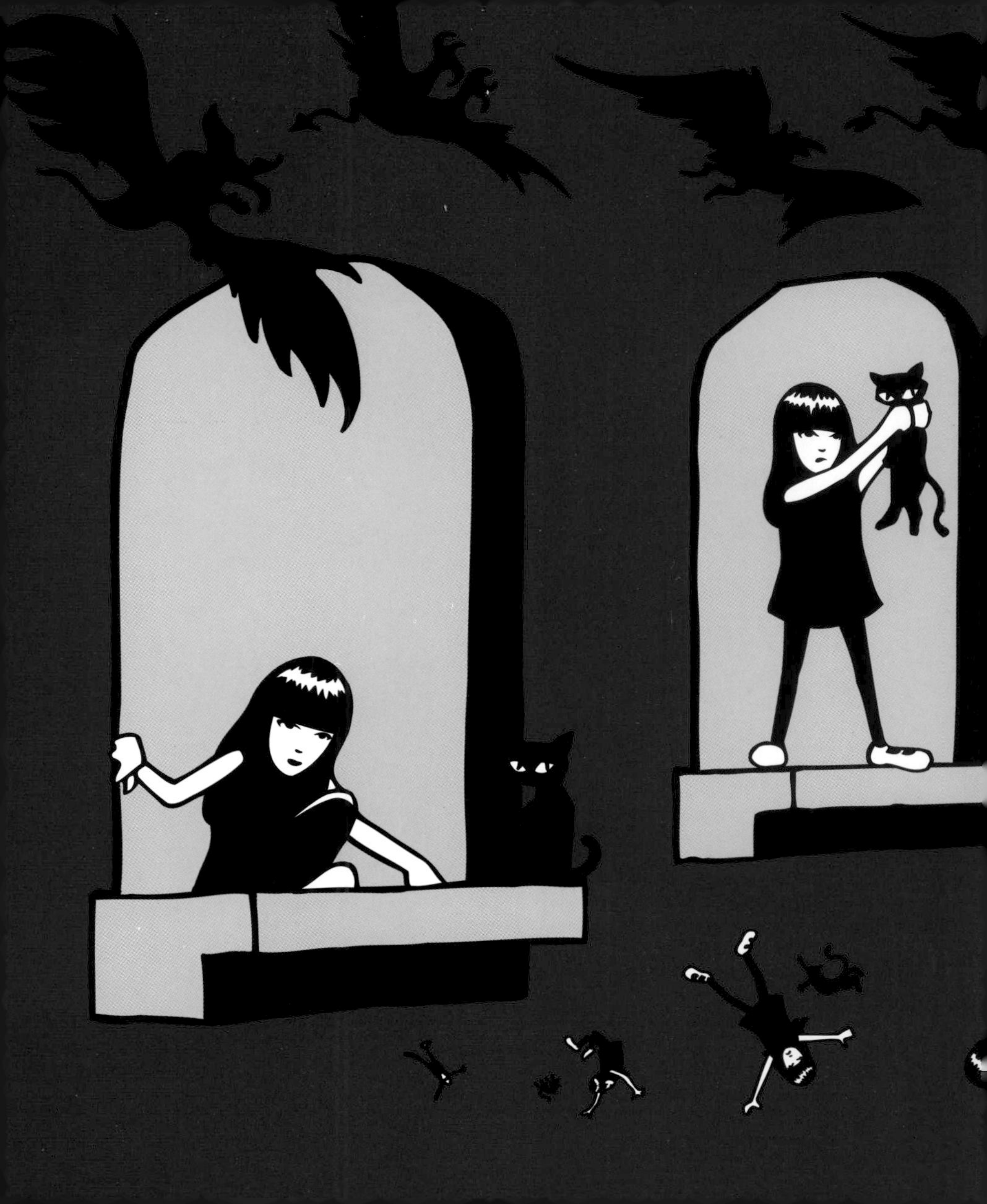

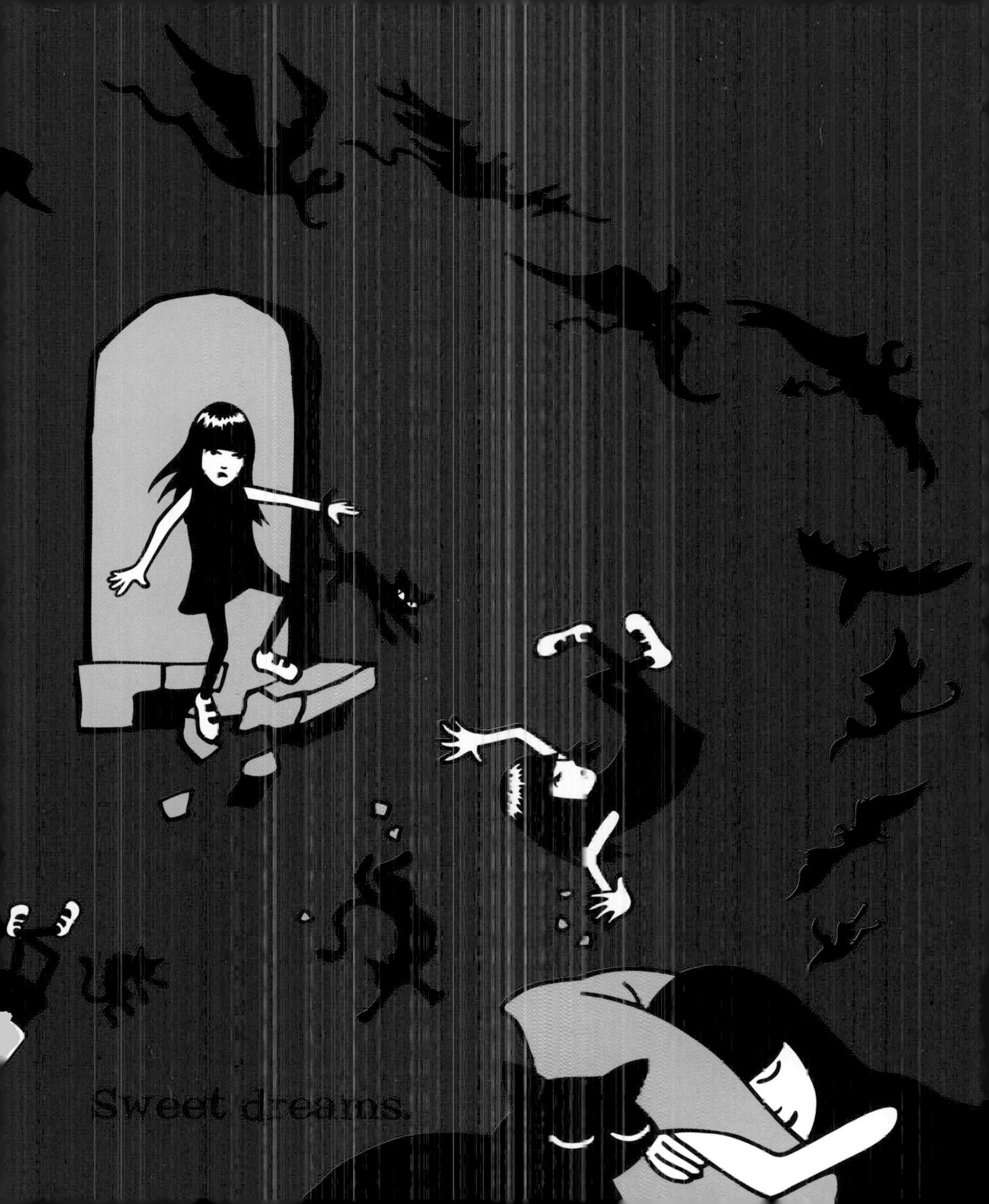
Sweet dreams.

Emily holds the future in her own hands

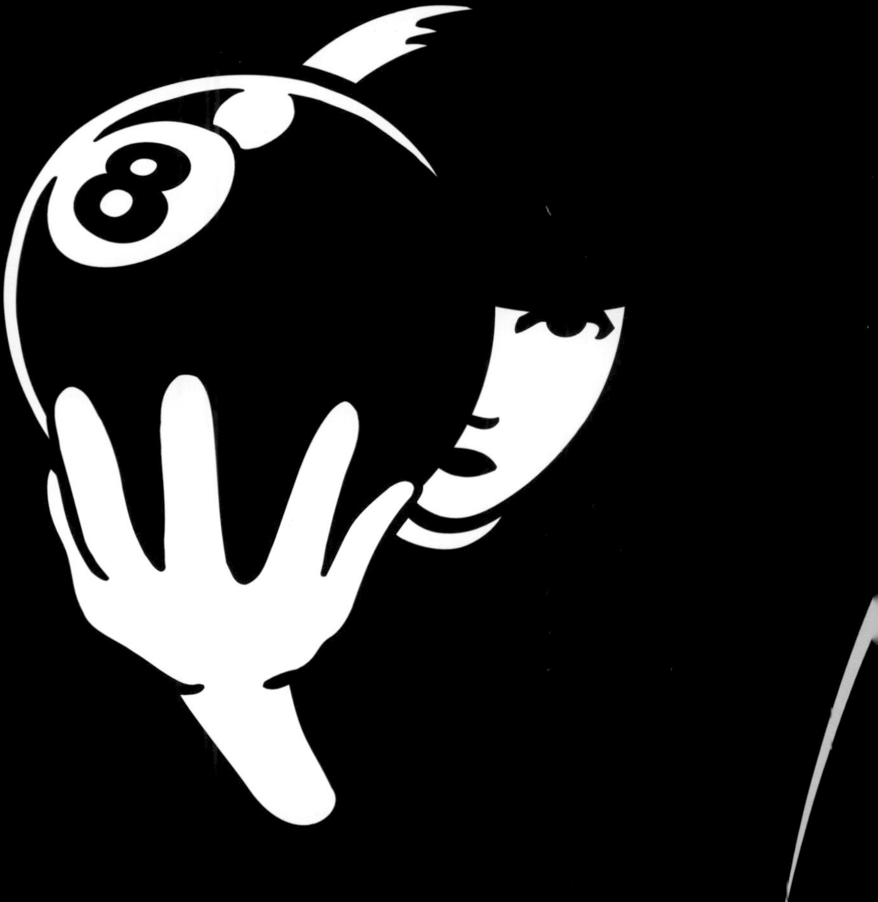

No future

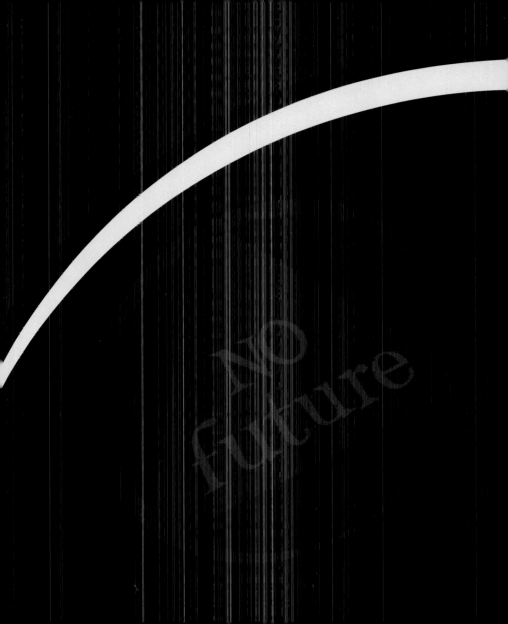

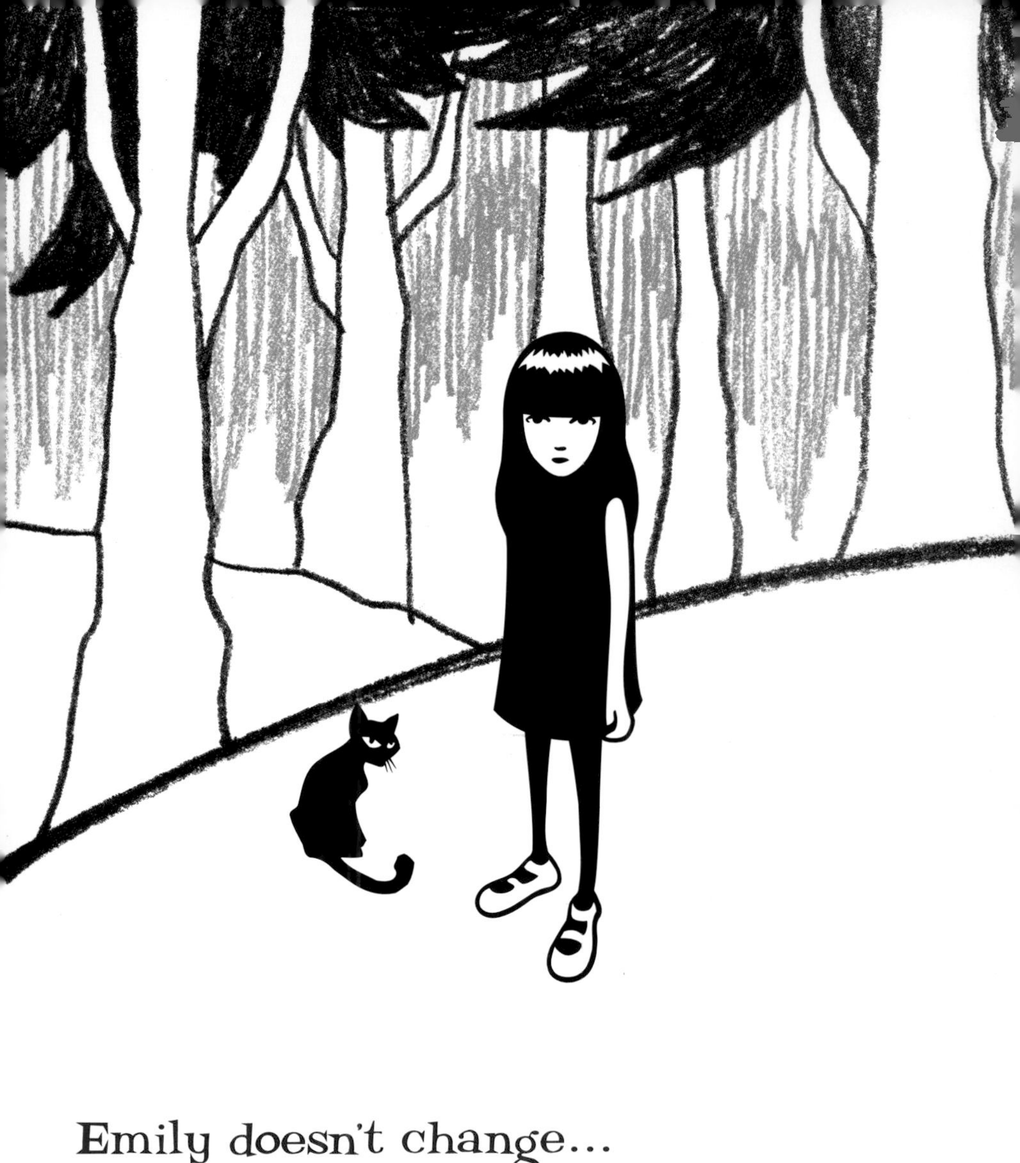

Emily doesn't change...

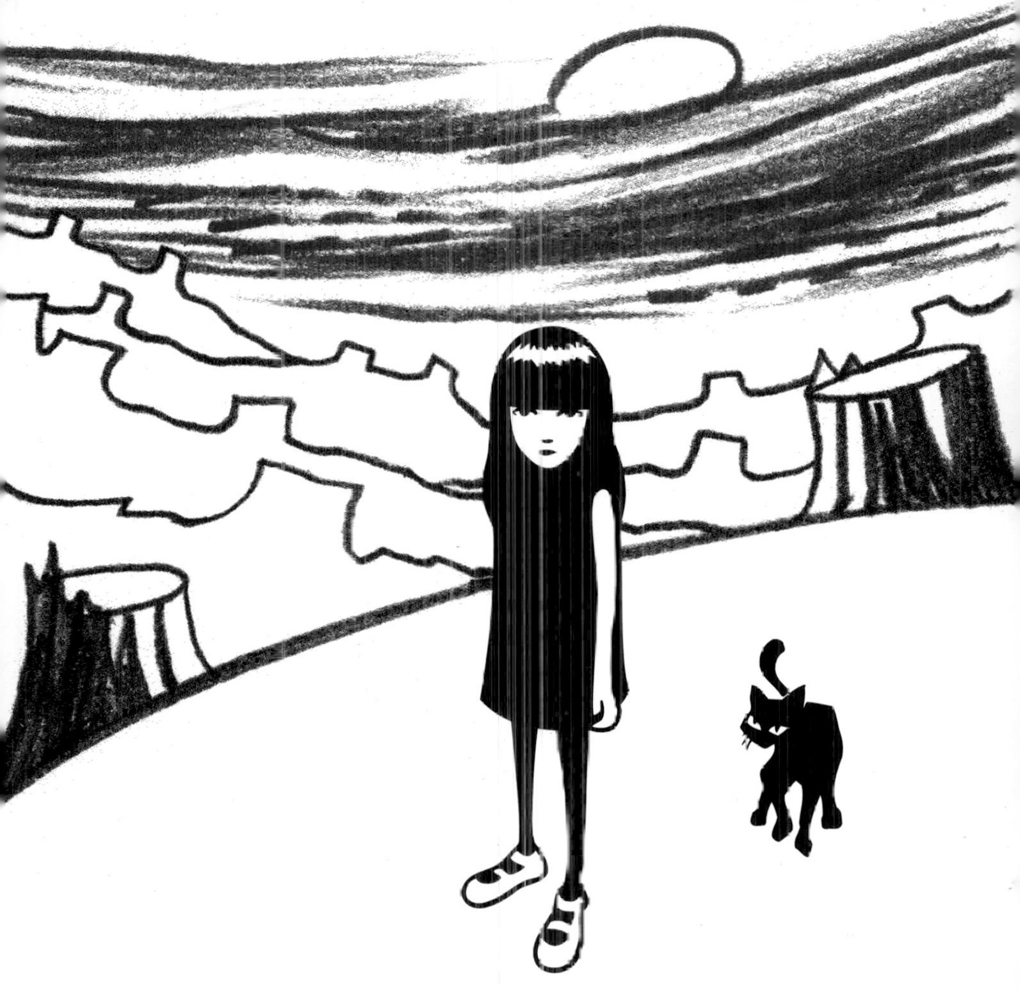

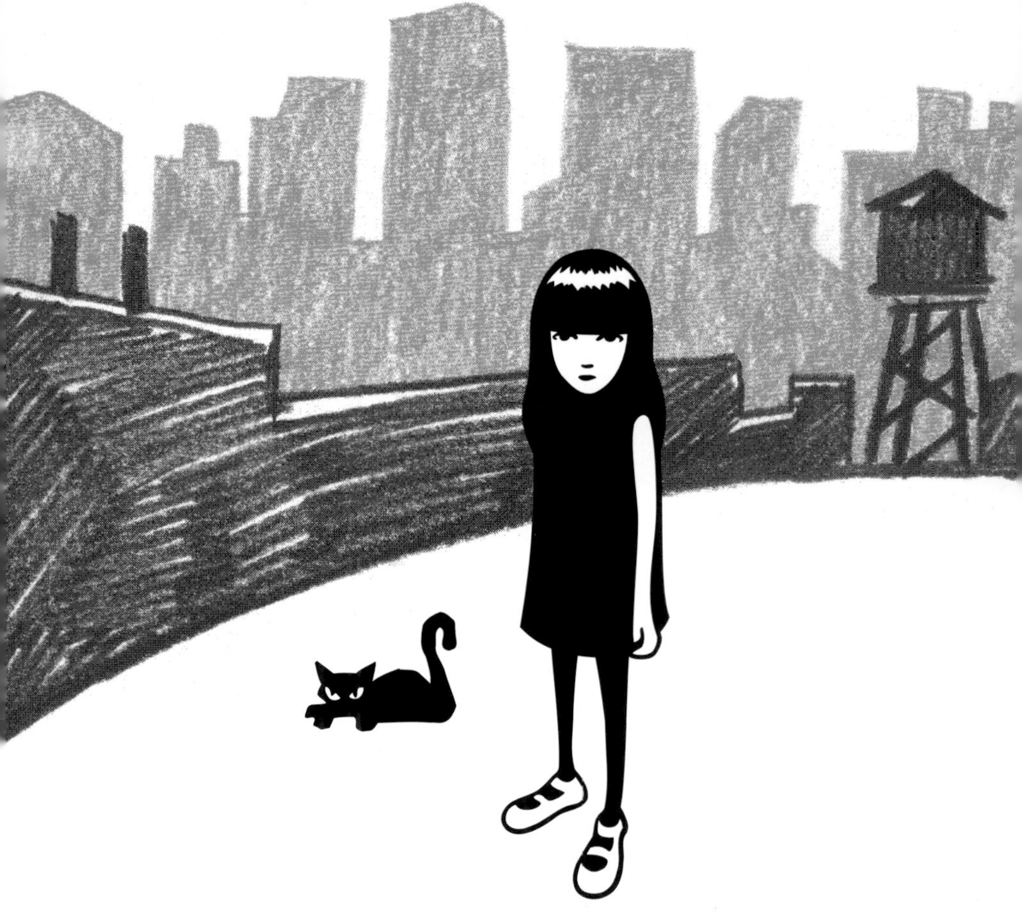

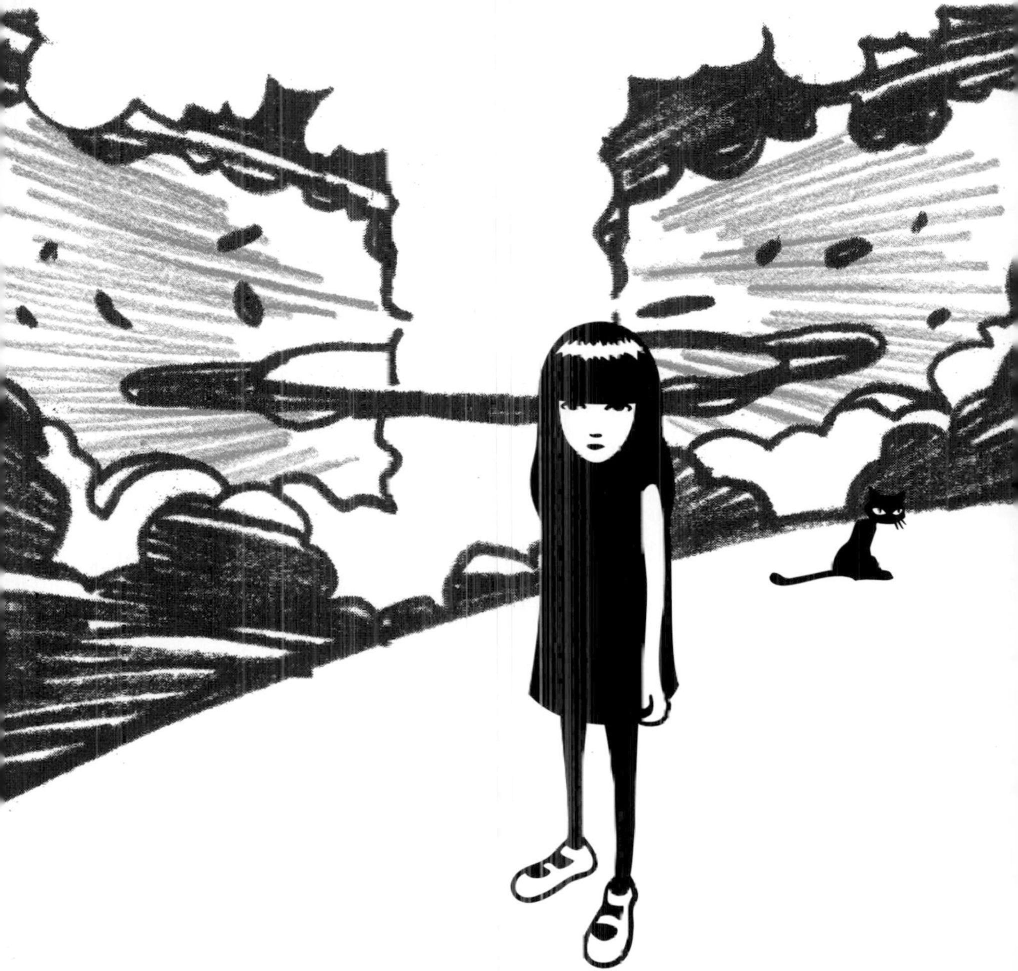

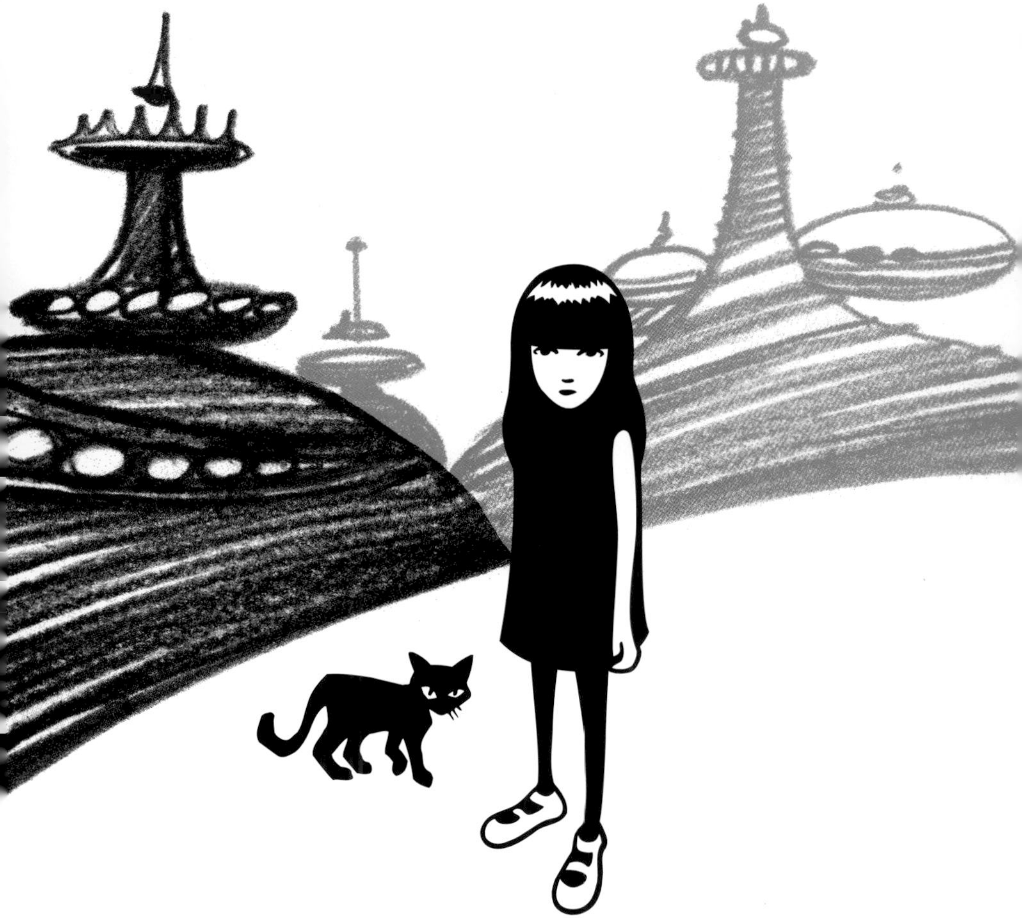

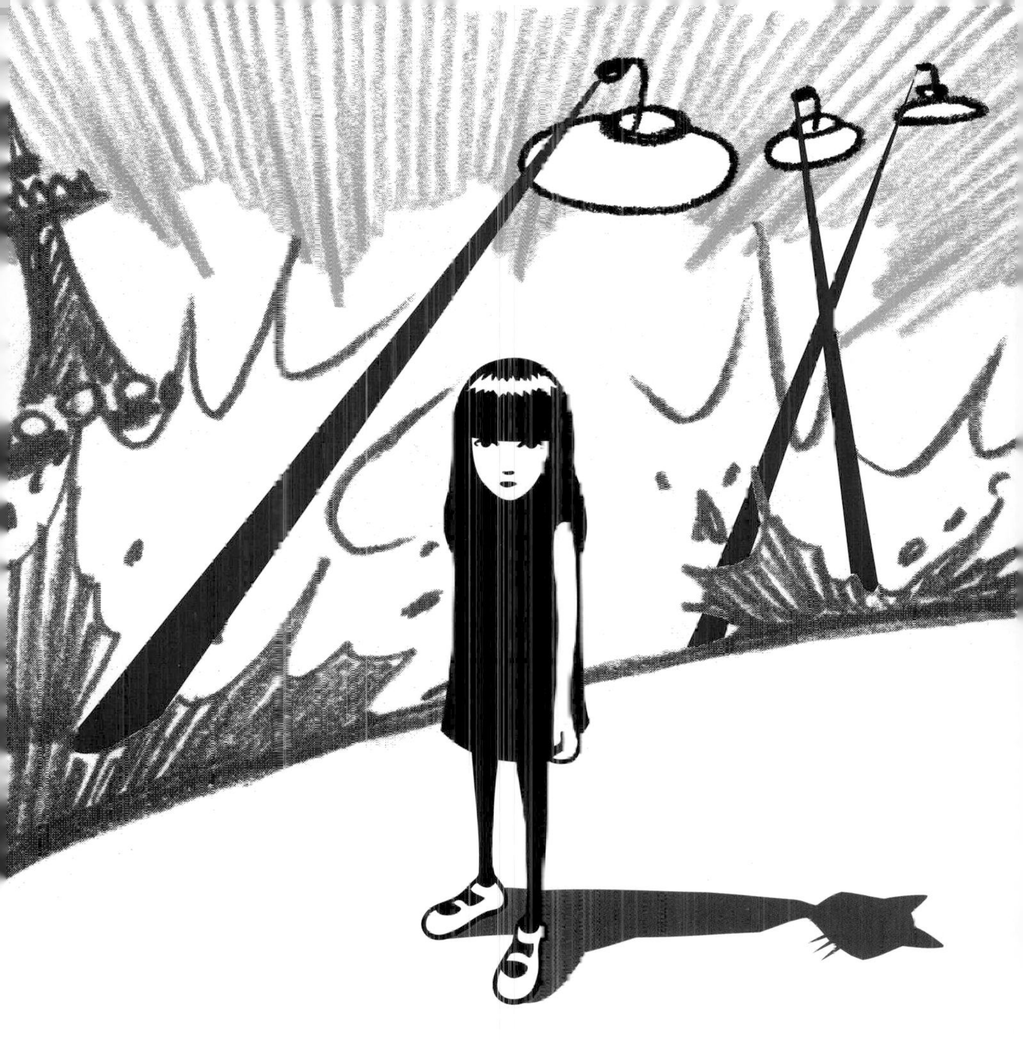

...she's always strange.

Special thanks to:

the Posse

Sabbath

Lives by his own rules.
Says "dude" a lot.

NeeChee

A Nihilist. He rarely
looks you in the eye.

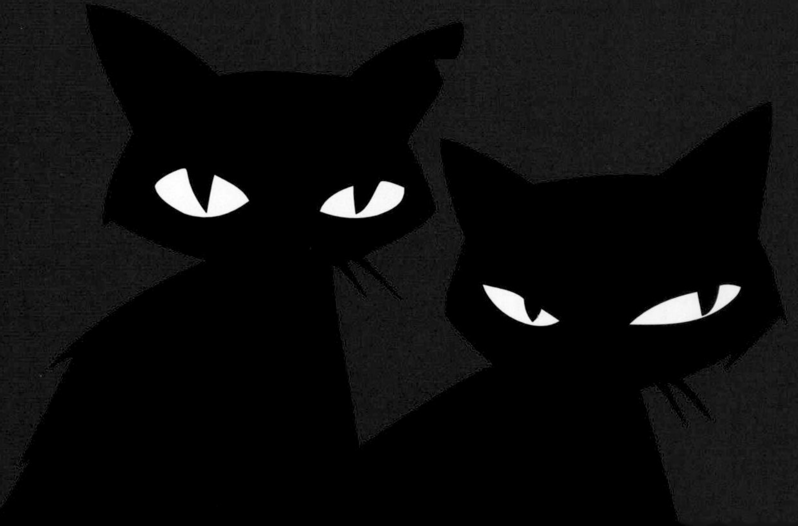

Miles

A creative genius. He's
the fastest cat in town.

Mystery

Emily's senior cat. What she says goes!
Voted "most likely to draw blood."

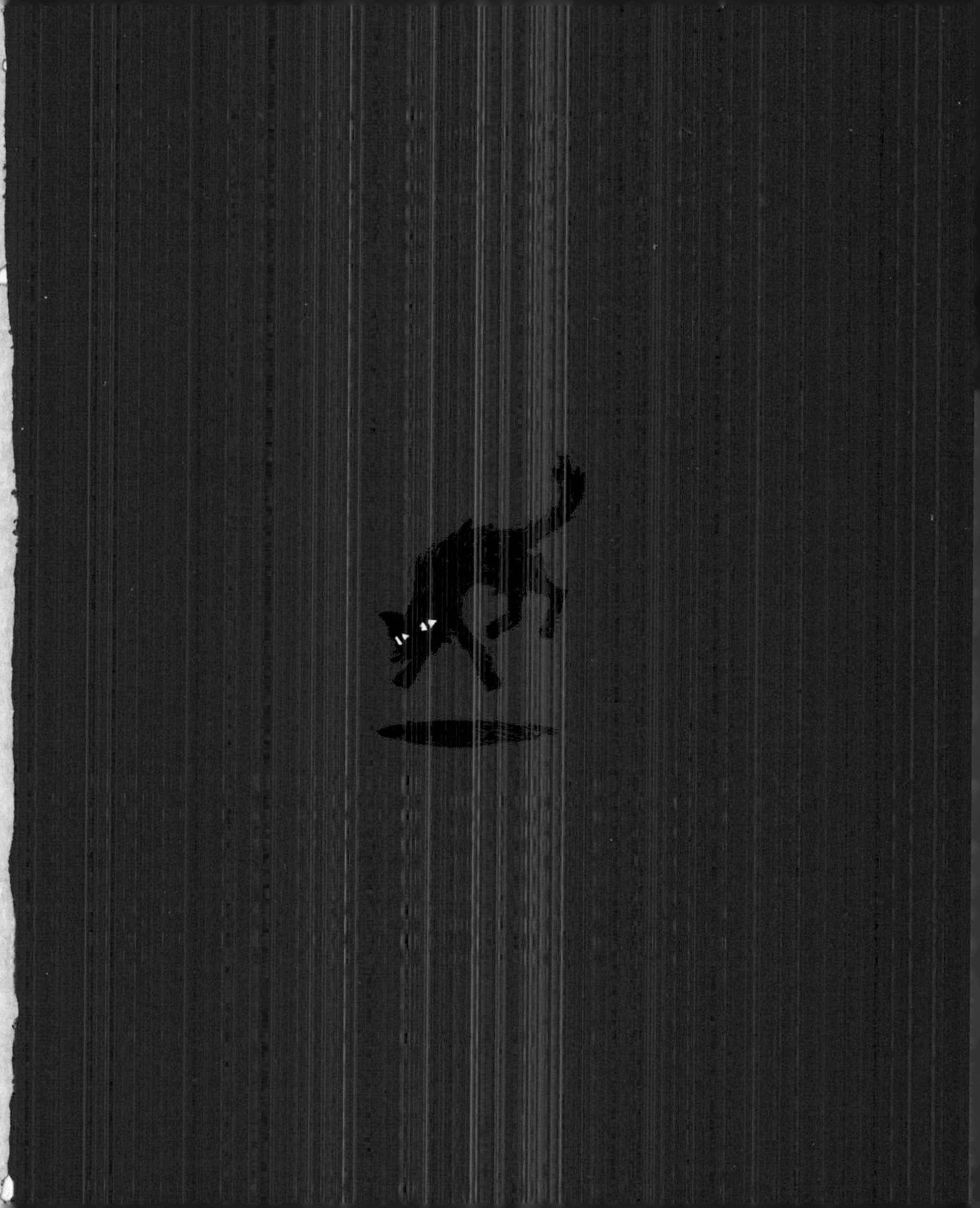